LANGUAGE, DISCOURSE, SOCIETY
General Editors: Stephen Heath, Colin MacCabe and Denise Riley

Published

Stanley Aronowitz
THE CRISIS IN HISTORICIAL MATERIALISM: Class, Politics and Culture in Marxist Theory
SCIENCE AS POWER: Discourse and Ideology in Modern Society

Mikkel Borch-Jacobsen
THE FREUDIAN SUBJECT

Norman Bryson
VISION AND PAINTING: The Logic of the Gaze

Teresa de Lauretis
ALICE DOESN'T: Feminism, Semiotics and Cinema
FEMINIST STUDIES/CRITICAL STUDIES (*editor*)
TECHNOLOGIES OF GENDER: Essays on Theory, Film and Fiction

Mary Ann Doane
THE DESIRE TO DESIRE: The Woman's Film of the 1940s

Alan Durant
CONDITIONS OF MUSIC

Jane Gallop
FEMINISM AND PSYCHOANALYSIS: The Daughter's Seduction

Peter Gidal
UNDERSTANDING BECKETT: A Study of Monologue and Gesture in the Works of Samuel Beckett

Peter Goodrich
LEGAL DISCOURSE: Studies in Linguistics, Rhetoric and Legal Analysis

Paul Hirst
ON LAW AND IDEOLOGY

Ian Hunter
CULTURE AND GOVERNMENT: The Emergence of Literary Education

Andreas Huyssen
AFTER THE GREAT DIVIDE: Modernism, Mass Culture and Postmodernism

Nigel Leask
THE POLITICS OF IMAGINATION IN COLERIDGE'S CRITICAL THOUGHT

Michael Lynn-George
EPOS: WORD, NARRATIVE AND THE *ILIAD*

Colin MacCabe
JAMES JOYCE AND THE REVOLUTION OF THE WORD
THE TALKING CURE: Essays on Psychoanalysis and Language (*editor*)

Louis Marin
PORTRAIT OF THE KING

Christian Metz
PSYCHOANALYSIS AND CINEMA:The Imaginary Signifier

Jean-Claude Milner
FOR THE LOVE OF LANGUAGE

Jeffrey Minson
GENEALOGIES OF MORALS: Nietzsche, Foucault, Donzelot and the Eccentricity of Ethics

Laura Mulvey
VISUAL AND OTHER PLEASURES

Douglas Oliver
POETRY AND NARRATIVE IN PERFORMANCE

Michel Pêcheux

LANGUAGE, SEMANTICS AND IDEOLOGY

Jean-Michel Rabaté
LANGUAGE, SEXUALITY AND IDEOLOGY IN EZRA POUND'S *CANTOS*

Denise Riley
'AM I THAT NAME?': Feminism and the Category of 'Women' in History

Jacqueline Rose
THE CASE OF PETER PAN OR THE IMPOSSIBILITY OF CHILDREN'S FICTION

Brian Rotman
SIGNIFYING NOTHING: The Semiotics of Zero

Michael Ryan
POLITICS AND CULTURE: Working Hypotheses for a Post-Revolutionary Society

James A. Snead and Cornel West
SEEING BLACK: A Semiotics of Black Culture in America

Raymond Tallis
NOT SAUSSURE: A Critique of Post-Saussurean Literary Theory

David Trotter
CIRCULATION: Defoe, Dickens and the Economies of the Novel
THE MAKING OF THE READER: Language and Subjectivity in Modern American, English and Irish Poetry

Carmel West
THE AMERICAN EVASION OF PHILOSOPHY: A Genealogy of Pragmatism

Peter Womack
IMPROVEMENT AND ROMANCE: Constructing the Myth of the Highlands

Forthcoming

James Donald
A SENTIMENTAL EDUCATION: Essays on Schooling and Popular Culture

Stephen Heath
FILM ANALYSIS: 'Touch of Evil'

Rod Mengham
CONTEMPORARY BRITISH POETICS

Jeffrey Minson
PERSONAL POLITICS AND ETHICAL STYLE

Denise Riley
POETS ON POETICS

Series Standing Order

If you would like to receive future titles in this series as they are published, you can make use of our standing order facility. To place a standing order please contact your bookseller or, in case of difficulty, write to us at the address below with your name and address and the name of the series. Please state with which title you wish to begin your standing order. (If you live outside the United Kingdom we may not have the rights for your area, in which case we will forward your order to the publisher concerned.)

Customer Services Department, Macmillan Distribution Ltd, Houndmills, Basingstoke, Hampshire, RG21 2XS, England

For the Love of Language

Jean-Claude Milner

Translated and introduced by Ann Banfield

MACMILLAN

Originally published as *L'amour de la
langue* by Editions du Seuil, 1978

English translation first published by
The Macmillan Press Ltd 1990

Published by
THE MACMILLAN PRESS LTD
Houndmills, Basingstoke, Hampshire RG212XS
and London
Companies and representatives
throughout the world

Printed in Hong Kong

British Library Cataloguing in Publication Data
Milner, Jean-Claude
For the love of language. — (Language,
discourse, society series).
1. Linguistics. Theories
I. Title   II. Series   III. L'amour de la
langue. *English*
410′1
ISBN 0–333–40878–0

Contents

Introduction:
What do Linguists Want?

THE AGE OF LINGUISTICS

A characteristic feature of our recent intellectual history was the conjunction of a universal valorisation of theoretical discourse in an array of disciplines ranging from the so-called 'human' sciences to poetics and psychoanalysis and the simultaneous elevation of linguistics to the status of model for the construction of theories and methodologies in these disciplines. Linguists, so often the very type of Carlyle's Dryasdust the scholar, embodiment of an obscure and irrelevant learning, had, as a consequence, briefly and with some bewilderment, found themselves, starting in the mid-1960s, intellectual cult figures, rubbing shoulders with artists, writers, and actors in the fashionable salons. One could invoke Chomsky descending the stage of the Beverly Hilton in 1971 in the company of Jane Fonda and other anti-war activists, commenting, in the face of a dozen news photographers, 'It's just like *La Dolce Vita*'.[1] Or Jakobson flying the Concorde (in a plane also carrying Princess Grace) to lecture at the Collège de France before an audience whose size was only equalled – or so a janitor told him – by Bergson's. The period when the elaboration of theories outside science itself was on the agenda and linguistics furnished the model for that project is now past. Once more linguists find themselves consigned to the fate of Proust's 'professor at the Sorbonne' Brichot, etymologising in Mme Verdurin's salon, ludicrous, 'too pedantic', their discourse grown boring; like him, their 'words no longer carried, having to overcome a hostile silence or disagreeable echoes; what had altered was not the things . . . said but the acoustics of the room and the attitude of the audience . . . difference of opinion, or of system' making them 'appear to other people absurd or old-fashioned'.[2]

To linguists, the pronouncements of these other disciplines, analogising from linguistics, had seemed, in turn, equally puzzling. What a structural anthropology and a structuralist poetics, a semiology and a Lacanian psychoanalysis claimed to take from linguistics was largely unrecognisable to the linguist. The relation between linguist and non-linguist was asymmetrical, non-reciprocal. The linguist as such had no need for these other disciplines; the goals of linguistics were sufficient and self-contained. In the 1960s and 1970s, the real discoveries and successes of the various linguistic paradigms – and most notably and recently, of transformational grammar – the productivity of their arguments provided linguists with intellectual projects, an intellectual labour, generating excitement and the promise of significant breakthroughs. Linguistics had not reached any impasse leading it to look beyond itself for indications as to how to proceed. (That individual linguists may have is irrelevant.) To add to this asymmetry, structural linguistics, particularly American structural linguistics – focused as it was on the study of languages such as American Indian languages, for which there were no written texts – and after it, transformational grammar, particularly in the United States, had largely severed their ties with *belles lettres*. The nineteenth-century philologist, trained in various largely Indo-European and Semitic languages, both ancient and modern, was perforce familiar with literary and historical texts and the scholarship surrounding them; the contemporary linguist might be more likely to be trained in field work in anthropology or in symbolic logic, and hence to be little inclined to take an interest in those disciplines looking to linguistics for a model, structural anthropology excepted.

The linguist and the non-linguist interested by linguistics thus could hardly be said to meet as equal partners in an exchange – that dream of an interdisciplinarity. Indeed, the self-sufficiency of linguists, the non-reciprocity of their relation to literary theory, semiology and psychoanalysis, made them briefly the envy of these other disciplines. It was a kind of unrequited love of which linguistics was the object, a linguistics, moreover, which often – at least from the linguist's point of view – seemed to have little to do with the linguistics of linguists. Perhaps the most extreme version of this non-meeting was that between Chomskyan transformational grammar, that most formal of linguistics, and Lacanian psychoanalysis, the most enigmatic celebration of the linguistic model, and its dramatic enactment took the form of a dinner which brought together Chomsky and Lacan, arranged by the mediator Jakobson, with Lacan as suitor.

The truth is that the discourse of linguistics had never been anything but perplexing and finally came to seem to the non-linguist irrelevant, irritating, boring. The death of linguistics was hence repeatedly proclaimed,[3] for now that non-linguists had ceased to think about linguistics, how could its continued existence be anything but an anachronism? Yet it persisted, apparently impervious to the demands or wishes of other disciplines that it concern itself with something other than it is. From seeming the keystone supporting a period's characteristic thinking, the linguistic model has become the gravestone marking a discarded set of assumptions. The question that arises in the aftermath is: which is now rendered more strange by the changeableness of intellectual fashion – that linguistics should have ever had an appeal to any but the few, or that it should remain ultimately so little understood?

The course of linguistics in this post-linguistic world is tied to that of language itself. It was the universal recognition of the centrality of language which supposedly explained the elevation of the linguistic model. Herein lies the original source of misunderstanding between linguist and non-linguist, in the referent of that term 'language'. It was not 'as a language'[4] that linguistics was asked to approach language, but as something else – a system of signs, a system of communication, an image or mask of thought. For this reason, it was not a love of language *per se* which led these other disciplines to question linguistics. Yet it is precisely English or French or Arabic as a language that interests linguistics. The object of linguistics was then not what non-linguists thought or wished it to be, the universal key to knowledge. A passion that once united a generation now divided it. Had linguistics turned out to be nothing but the hated grammar of the school, refusing to make language the servant of man, the tool of communication, to make it conform to the needs and expectations of semioticians, literary critics, ethnologists, but instead making students of language, like the schoolchild, serve language? In that case, was the universal boredom with the subject of linguistics the final comment on the project which had based itself on the science of language? If the scientific model had failed to be extended to other domains, did that reflect on the scientific status of linguistics itself? Had linguistics finally made no contribution that could be comprehensible or meaningful to any but a linguist? Was the linguist possessed of a knowledge misunderstood and unappreciated by those who had outgrown an infatuation with linguistics and, by extension, with language itself, yet unable to communicate that knowledge to anyone who does not become – as is not the case for every discipline – likewise a linguist?

GO, DUMB-BORN BOOK

'Boredom', Roland Barthes tells us, 'is not simple'. 'Boredom is not far from bliss; it is bliss seen from the shores of pleasure', he explains from a vantage point in time when his enthusiasm for linguistics had receded to that distant shore of a former passion.[5]

The fact that boredom with something is only the state of having fallen out of love with it makes it no less difficult to comprehend the former state, as we know from Proust. But when it is a case of being left stranded on that other shore and wishing to convey a still felt excitement shared by few or none, the impossible task of communicating that excitement to the bored, of explaining what it is that linguists are after to those with completely different expectations of the goals of linguistics, takes on the dimensions of a self-justification on the part of one condemned to the modern equivalent of a heresy trial: condemned to being ignored and passed over in silence.

It is this little book which audaciously, flying in the face of the real difference between linguistics and its erstwhile suitors, is sent to bring into contact what nevertheless remains distinct and different, two different conceptions of language, the linguistic and the non-linguistic, like Proust's little wasp 'transversally' fertilising the otherwise non-communicating flowers of the Duchesse de Guermantes' orchid and causing 'the partitioned sexes to communicate', 'a communication resulting . . . from what does not communicate'[6] And it does so in the name of two approaches to language which could be no further apart: Chomskyan transformational grammar and Lacanian psychoanalysis. For like Tiresias, this book encapsulates a heterologia; it speaks from two experiences, from the subjective possession of two knowledges normally not residing in the same individual. The fortuitous meeting of these two alien knowledges (the un-English plural is required to express their discreteness) within the pages of *For the Love of Language* is uniquely determined by the intellectual biography of its author; Chomskyan linguist trained as well in the ancient languages of the comparative grammarian, Milner was also associated with the Ecole Freudienne.[7]

It is the coexistence of two discontinuous domains of knowledge which have not been assimilated one to the other that can be read in Jean-Claude Milner's bibliography as the most apparent and constant principle in what, since the publication of the French original of *For the Love of Language* in 1978, has become a developing *oeuvre*. From a work of pure formal syntax like *De la Syntaxe à l'Interprétation* (1978) or texts including formal syntactic analyses like *Arguments Linguistiques* (1973) and *Ordres et Raisons de Langue* (1982) to not only *For the Love of Language*, which appeared in Lacan's series, Le Champ Freudien, but also its political companion piece, *Les Noms Indistincts* (1983), published in the Connexions du Champ Freudien, along with the interpretive logic or 'detections' of *Détections Fictives* (1985) and a recent book on the alexandrine, co-authored with François Regnault, *Dire le Vers* (1987), the alternate points of view are adopted, now sequentially, now by turns within the same work.[8] Always, however, the differences between the two domains of thought are maintained. For to possess two such radically unconnected knowledges is not to connect them; it is above all to recognise more than anyone their essential difference and to live, like the Duchess's orchid, with discontinuous parts of knowledge.

Such a divided state is a familiar one – that called the 'modern' consciousness. Its appearance is consonant with the rise of science. That is, the modern subject of science cannot unite a plurality of 'knowledges' which English expresses only by the word 'sciences' into that imaginary figure known as the Renaissance man.[9] It is not that the scientist may not have access to more than one branch of knowledge, some scientific, some not; it is that science, in searching for 'scientific' explanation, must reject what Bertrand Russell identifies as the mystic belief in 'the apparent revelation of the oneness of all things'.[10] That mystic and all-embracing oneness is the contrary of what Milner calls, after Lacan, the One; the latter notion partakes rather of the features of that 'atomism' or 'pluralism' which Russell elsewhere counterposes to the single, mystic One, the 'common-sense belief that there are many separate things'.[11] For Lacan's One has the property of being countable – 'one by one'. There is no once for all, but a countable series.

Science registers most acutely the limits or boundaries of knowledge; the condition for its existence is the recognition of its partiality. The resultant rejection of the belief in unity is the foundation of what Milner calls 'the ethic of science' (p. 79). That ethic, as we shall see, is based on a renunciation. It is not simply the renouncing of the goal for science to embrace all knowledge. It is also the recognition that the different parts of an individual's knowledge cannot simply be added up into an interconnected whole and, correlatively, that the different objective spheres of knowledge cannot be integrated. It is perhaps predictable that linguistics today should stand at the frontiers of science and non-science, bearing witness to the impossible unity of knowledge – in the lack of comprehension it meets with everywhere, in the failure to see that it cannot be found wanting as a science for not having answers to all the questions put to it. For its knowledge is the newest science, unique in carrying formal representation and argumentation not into the external, physical world, but into an internal, non-physical one: the speaker's knowledge, which Chomsky calls 'linguistic competence' (pp. 54–5). The validity of its claim to scientificity is thus dependent on its refusal to comment on all *uses* of language. The punishment for that refusal has been a universal scepticism denying any theoretical coherence to the limited claims of linguistics precisely because there exist aspects of language it cannot explain.

THE EXPERIENCE OF SCIENCE

What is perhaps unexpected is that the linguist's knowledge as linguist is not contaminated by this universal scepticism. Here lies the core of Milner's argument from which so much else is derived: the linguist's conviction is rooted in an experience unique to linguists among the researchers in the 'human' sciences – and here Milner, speaking for himself, means to articulate something which other linguists, but not necessarily others than linguists, will immediately recognise, though it be only privately and though they might find the language in which it is articulated foreign. This is what one might call 'the experience of science' – something more than its simple practice, but requiring that practice. It is on the basis of that experience that linguists are led to what they think of as 'linguistic discoveries' comparable to those of any physical science. Having had that experience, via what procedures they might not be able to say, some of them might, with hindsight, turn to scrutinise in order to make explicit the implicit logic of the arguments they came to follow. Thus is science brought into line with Proust's formula for the work of art that the intelligence comes after a prior experience,[12] reversing the priority of methodology over discovery which characterised the model of science of a structural linguistics, and which a structuralist poetics found in that linguistic model.[13] It is its quality as experience – albeit a mental one – that confers its privacy, its incommunicability on the knowledge which is the content of linguistics and motivates the otherwise strange term Milner chooses for it: the *jouissance* of the linguist, that word which in ordinary French means not simply 'pleasure' but can designate the climax of the sexual act. *Jouissance* has been taken by Lacan to stand for a precise complex of notions; his seminar XX, entitled *Encore*, takes *jouissance* as its point of departure, a *jouissance* qualified as 'feminine' and explicitly contrasted with pleasure, the specifically female orgasm being emblematic of what interests Lacan in *la jouissance*. It is not simply a state, like pleasure, but an event, hence occurring in time (even if instantaneously), hence repeatable (the possible 'encore'), but also, like any real event, one which may or may not take place. That it has cannot, moreover, be determined by outward signs; it can be known only by the subject experiencing it, incapable of explaining, of communicating it, the *je jouis* like a sexual *cogito*. To capture this idea of *jouissance* as an event rather than a state, I have rendered the word in English by 'the thrill' or 'the thrill of pleasure' and the verb by 'to take pleasure.' But 'the thrill of pleasure' should not be understood as the state of pleasure nor should 'to take pleasure' be understood as 'to have pleasure'.

The linguist's thrill lies, however, in the experience of science: that is, it is attached to a theoretical knowledge, a particular kind which the word 'science' has come uniquely to denote. It is in the connection between linguistic theory and the experience in which it is arrived at that Milner locates the source of the misunderstanding linguistics has encountered. Of course, that theory is set down in the formal account which externalises it from the experience, the process of discovery and the theory not being the same and the former disappearing in the latter, along with the one who formulated the hypothesis. The enigmatic quality that surrounds linguistics as science is due not simply to its difficulty but to the fact that, although it is theoretical, it – like any real science – can be seized only through a research, an experience, whose sign has traditionally been not cognitive but exclamatory: a 'eureka!' that is more than any mere heuristic, as *je pense* exceeds 'it is thought'. To have that experience is already to be a linguist, even if for a moment (p. 124). This is why the formal study of linguistics, like any of the positive sciences, crucially involves the assignment of problems, whereby the student is forced artificially to have the thrill connected with their solution, to repeat under idealised conditions insuring success the discoveries that make up the history of this science.

But *For the Love of Language* is no introduction to linguistics designed as a substitute for that knowledge gained only through an apprenticeship in practice.[14] It is an attempt to reveal to the non-linguist the existence of an experience of science at the heart of linguistics in order ultimately to say in what way that experience is attached to linguistics' legitimacy as a science – in other words, to defend the profession of linguistics before a tribunal whose accusations and sentence amount to the same thing: found guilty of the same boredom they are subjected to – the non-linguist's – linguists are dismissed, pronounced useless. But in their defence, Milner cannot merely communicate this experience, any more than for Lacan the woman can speak of her *jouissance*. For one thing, what it involved is afterwards as inaccessible for the one who has undergone it as for the one who has not. Milner takes recourse then to a version of Proust's retrospective analytic method, set forth in *Contre Sainte-Beuve*. There, Proust argues, it is intellectual analysis which is required to establish the second-best status of this analysis subsequent to experience; it is only this analysis which is able to discern the importance of what has preceded it.[15]. But in Milner this scrutiny takes an unexpected – if, as we shall see, a not entirely unprecedented – form, aiming in part to isolate and analyse the experience, and in part to define the status and specific nature of this 'science' linguistics claims to be. This dual perspective on both the linguist and linguistics accounts for the peculiar form of this little book, so difficult to classify, at once a psychoanalysis of the linguist as a subject of science and a philosophy of that science.

CONFESSIO AMANTIS LINGUAE

A science contains in its history an experience whose place in that history must be understood if the science is to be understood. Thus, it cannot be minimised or forgotten that the author of *For the Love of Language* is a practising linguist; and this book, which proceeds in a way so unlike linguistic practice, should in no way be construed as a rejection of that practice. Rather, in defending it, the book is shaped by the private character of an experience: it is an apologia – *pro curriculo vitae suae* – making in an impersonal form a personal statement, a confession of an attachment to a learning and its object. The particular impersonal form that is given to autobiographical material Milner identifies: it is a 'wild self-analysis', in the technical sense of Freud. That analysis originates in a fact Milner observes about himself so as to render it strange and in need of explanation: why is it that, when linguistics has ceased to retain the interest of so many, does he, so easily prey to boredom elsewhere, continue to find linguistics interesting?

The analysis and justification of a continuously renewed interest for a subject become unfashionable situates *For the Love of Language* with respect to certain other similarly conceived projects, without claiming them as sources. One of especial interest is Roland Barthes's *The Pleasure of the Text*, that apology for a persistent preference for the nineteenth-century novel which runs counter to the defence of modernism of his own earlier *Writing Degree Zero*. In it, Barthes evinces a surprise like Milner's at catching himself in an attachment. Although, unlike Milner, Barthes speaks specifically of pleasure and not its counterpart in Lacan's scheme, *jouissance* (there translated by Richard Howard as 'bliss'), the pleasure of Barthes's title, like the linguist's thrill, is that of one 'obsessed' by 'the letter', in contrast to the fetishist of the text, its paranoiac, its hysteric. In terms he pronounces 'could only be psychoanalytic',[16] the 'typology' of 'the readers of pleasure' catalogue among such obsessionals under the general heading of 'all those who love language (and not speech)', 'logophiles, authors, letter writers, linguists' (p. 21), or again, 'all the logophiles, linguists, semioticians, philologists: all those for whom language *returns*' (p. 63). What Barthes's category calls attention to, to the point of making it also strange and unaccounted for, is the very existence of a love of language unshared by the population of speakers and readers at large, a love which animated traditional grammar and, at times, even the schoolteacher, and which apparently was still felt by Barthes, but which is so generally replaced by boredom. Or something uglier boredom conceals. 'There is no sincere boredom', Barthes comments (p. 25). For the truth is, language as revealed by linguistics is disturbing to certain cherished beliefs of our culture and arouses a 'hatred' of language or the 'irritated regret that men are speaking' Milner invokes elsewhere.[17] Milner's text is thus a confession of a secret love for something fallen into disrepute, considered useless (and use is the supreme value) or even threatening.

Yet there remain some 'for whom language *returns*'. Barthes's deliberately emphasised psychoanalytic term '*returns*' echoes the title of perhaps the most important single text behind Milner's: Lacan's *Encore*. It is not simply that this seminar supplies an extended commentary on those of Lacan's terms which play a central role in *For the Love of Language* – besides *jouissance*, the very subject of *Encore*, the notions of *lalangue* and the *pas-tout*, used so crucially by Milner and whose translations we have yet to comment on, are all elaborated in *Encore*. Nor is it the trace that an earlier text of Milner's leaves in the transcription of the seminar for 10 April 1973 (p. 93), there titled 'The Position of the Linguist'.[18] This makes not only *For the Love of Language* point to *Encore*, but *Encore* to both *Arguments Linguistiques* and Milner himself as representative linguist.[19]

These links between *Encore* and *For the Love of Language* are obvious enough, but stopping there would miss the most important connection and the one least apparent to the English-speaking reader. In the brief commentary Lacan makes on Milner's presentation, he speaks of 'a certain number of ways of proceeding that we owe perhaps – I am speaking of myself – to nothing but a certain distance that we were from this rising science, when it believed that it could become just that, a science'.[20] The subject of linguistics as a science that we recognise as Milner's is perhaps not readily associated with Lacan's seminars and most especially not with *Encore*, which is known in English through the excerpted translation of Juliet Mitchell and Jacqueline Rose as a commentary on feminine sexuality.[21] Milner's subject that day was a quite specific and technical comparison between two schools of linguistics – Zellig Harris's structuralism and Noam Chomsky's transformational grammar – with respect to the homonymous notion of transformation in both, in order to compare them as two versions of science. If today Lacan is one of those invoked to dismiss attention from such questions in the name of 'post-structuralism', the current nominalism and scepticism, which advertises itself as the dismantling of all science and theoretical inquiry, a careful reading of *Encore* should be taken as a caution against the facile dismissal of the equation of linguistics and science. Rather, Lacan and Milner represent different workings out of a theory of science where linguistics is the science in question and where the existence of that science presents an explicit challenge to any nominalism with regard to language. If there is scepticism, it is directed toward a theory of science conceived as a preoccupation with a methodology whose assigned role is to define what any scientific research should be. Like all philosophy of science, this theory takes it as given that a distinctly scientific knowledge exists, and seeks rather to establish the criteria for identifying it and distinguishing it from non-scientific knowledge. These criteria receive their unique form, however, within a specifically French rationalist tradition. Determining the criteria for linguistics to qualify as a science is not Milner's ultimate destination, however; he directs his analysis toward the experience at the heart of science, to what it is to arrive at the knowledge which constitutes it for the one who qualifes as a scientist by virtue of it. But to follow Milner's itinerary, we must first try to situate ourselves at his starting point within the rationalist reading of science. In so doing, we will encounter other analogues for his project of a kind of 'psychoanalysis of objective knowledge'.[22]

THE EPISTEMOLOGY OF LINGUISTICS

This account of scientific knowledge is little known outside the French-speaking world and when it is, it is often misconstrued. The very term 'epistemology' of science by which it is identified as a separate discipline sets it apart from the philosophy of science deriving from British and Viennese logical empiricism more familiar in the English-speaking world.[23] In the latter tradition, epistemology and philosophy of science can be taken as mutually exclusive. An empiricist epistemology is understood to overlap with psychology, aiming to account for the knowledge of individual subjects, classically rooted in sense perception; philosophy of science, as its complement, seeks to define and validate a knowledge ideally independent of the subject: 'science'. Within this tradition, the primary concern has been to keep these two domains separate – that is, to justify a domain of knowledge independent of the knowing subject, although dependent on observation, primarily conceived as the evidence of the senses. In this sense, philosophy of science is an attempt to solve the problem of knowledge as it is formulated by empiricism. The essential question bearing on the putative bifurcation of knowledge concerns the validation of an objective knowledge of the physical world which pretends to speak empirically. All this is well known; I have tried only to reiterate in broad outline the characteristic approach of philosophy of science – and it is as such that I refer to the British and Viennese tradition–so that what is different in the epistemology of science emerges.

The differences of French epistemology of science reside, on the one hand, in a historical thesis – that marked by the notion of the break, perhaps traceable to Comte; and, on the other, in a rationalist conception of scientific knowledge as quite distinct from pre-scientific knowledge, developing a notion which itself is traceable to Pascal. Both share the conviction of the radical, indeed revolutionary, difference of scientific knowledge. This epistemology of science can be attached to certain names: Kojève, initially and not specifically linked to the sciences, Bachelard in a more idiosyncratic way, Duhem and Meyerson, Koyré, and, more recently for the human sciences, Foucault.[24] If these names are known in the English-speaking world, it is typically not in connection with a tradition of debate on a general theory of science; yet it is against the background of this theory that Milner's specific claims for linguistics must be understood.

It is the particular hypotheses of Alexandre Koyré that are built upon in *For the Love of Language*. In Koyré's epistemology, the bifurcation between scientific and non-scientific knowledge – what, in philosophy of science after Popper, the so-called 'demarcation criteria' are meant to characterise–takes the form of an 'epistemic break'[25] that is, a change which operates at the level of a set of theoretical assumptions. This break occurs for Koyré between Aristotelian and Galilean science. In his treatment of the rise of science Koyré has explicitly de-emphasised the role of observation in favour of what Lakatos has called 'metaphysical' research programmes.[26] It is theory which sets the goals of observation for Koyré.

Koyré's 'revolutionary' model of the rise of science has been given the widest circulation in English in Kuhn's *The Structure of Scientific Revolutions*.[27] As this emphasis on the priority of theory has been translated into an Anglo–American universe of discourse, with its pragmatist assumptions, a distortion of the notion of the theoretical takes place. In Kuhn's history of science, the theoretical is embodied in institutionalised disciplines, which substitute for independent criteria of evaluation; truth becomes 'truth by consensus'.' The resultant subordination of theory to external factors obscures the real originality of Koyré's conception of the new, Galilean science and his challenge to an empiricist emphasis on observation; all that remains of Koyré's history of science is the 'revolutionary' model – i.e., one that proceeds by ruptures.[28]

On the other hand, the priority of theory does not itself suffice to distinguish science from pre-scientific thought. Any account of the supplanting of ancient and medieval science by the new science must deal with the obvious role of the empirical in the development of scientific theory. The distinctive feature of Koyré's thesis, as the representative of a rationalist epistemology of science, lies at once in the particular formulation of the relative contributions of the theoretical and the empirical and in the conception of the empirical itself. These converge in Koyré's conception of 'Galilean' or modern science, which is of crucial relevance to Milner's epistemology of linguistics.

THE MATHEMATISATION OF THE REAL

For there to be science – i.e., Galilean science – in Koyré's account, theory must bring about the formalisation or mathematicisation of the empirical. That is, science is defined by the conjunction of two factors: the empirical and the mathematical – i.e., a mathematical writing. 'Indeed', Milner comments, 'Koyré always insisted on the radical novelty of the fact that mathematics could be connected with empiricity rather than eternity', with the contingent rather than the necessary. The form of this conjunction is expressed in the proposition 'the empirical is mathematicised'.[29]

The past participle 'mathematicised' suggests an achievement of the history of science. But there is not just an historically occurring mathematicisation of the empirical, as an imposition of form on matter. Koyré's claim, as Milner reads it, also involves the assumption of a prior condition permitting this mathematicisation: the empirical is discovered to be 'mathematicisable' – representable in a formal writing – where the adjective 'mathematicisable' designates a quality inherent in the empirical. Milner's formulation is the following': 'It is not its writing which establishes the One by convention, but on the contrary it is the latter which makes this writing possible' (p. 91–2). The operation of formally representing the empirical is thus not possible in any domain, but only where an empirical reality has properties subject to formalisation, and scientific discovery is the matching of an empiricity and a mathematical formula, of extracting, abstracting, the mathematical from the empirical. The mathematical writing is never thought to impose a form on a formless portion of the real; theory becomes a tool for representing a regularity, a law of the physical world. It is precisely in the discovery of a portion of empirical reality fitting the mathematical writing that, as we shall see, the experience of science lies.

THE ENCOUNTER WITH THE REAL

The empirical for Koyré, however, coincides in no simple way with raw experience, common sense observation, or sense data. What, then, constitutes the empirical for him? Milner's answer is the following: 'Koyré never defined explicitly what he meant by the empirical, but it is plausible to define that notion in the following way:

> In order to be considered as empirical, a statement should meet two conditions: (1) the state of things it refers to should be directly or indirectly representable in space and time; (2) it should be possible to think of the state of things it refers to as different from what it is'.[30]

It is the second condition – the possibility of imagining the state of affairs referred to by an empirical statement as different from what it is – which permits the most characteristically rationalist definition of the empirical, placing it under the sign of the contingent. 'In the philosophical tradition', Milner comments, 'condition (2) has something to do with contingence and also with synthetic vs analytic'.[31] Condition (2) formulates a philosophical notion that has had a special and persistent role in French thought, under various incarnations and names, from Pascal to Lacan. In *For the Love of Language*, Milner connects it with Saussure's notion of arbitrariness, attributing the term 'contingence' to Lacan and 'chance' to Mallarmé. Milner's vocabulary supplies another term: a 'meeting' or 'encounter'. These words, as verb or noun, recur again and again in *For the Love of Language*; as verb its characteristic object is that key term we have yet to comment on: the real. It is in Lacan that the real receives this explicit formulation in terms of the chance encounter. There the concept is developed by contrast with the other two terms of a triad–the imaginary and the symbolic – as well as in contradistinction to the notion 'reality'. Of the three terms of Lacan's triad, the notion of the real has received little attention in the Anglo–American context, with as a result a concomitant shifting of the other two terms toward the same nominalism that marks Kuhn's misreading of Koyré.[32] The imaginary and the symbolic are not grounds for discounting the existence of the real; this is the force of Lacan's formula that 'the Real always returns to its place'.[33]

Central to Lacan's elaboration of the Real, set forth at length in *The Four Fundamental Concepts of Psychoanalysis*,[34] is that of 'the encounter with the Real', a phrase Lacan himself emphasises. The context in which the notion is there introduced can guide us in understanding and assessing its import and correct the already observed tendency to push Lacan toward either nominalism or idealism. Lacan opens the fifth session of 12 February 1964 by denying explicitly that psychoanalysis, contrary to a common assumption, can be taken 'to lead in the direction of idealism'. The basis of that denial is, moreover, a consideration of 'the experience of psycho-analysis'. It is in the context of this denial that the term 'real' is introduced: 'No praxis is more oriented towards that which, at the heart of experience, is the kernel of the real than psycho-analysis' (p. 53).

It is, then, in this context of a question raised about the epistemological status of psychoanalysis as both a theory and a practice that Lacan links the real to the *chance encounter*,[35] to 'something that occurs . . . *as if by chance*' (p. 54, Lacan's emphasis). This encounter, as one 'to which we are always called', is not conjured up by the subject but enters from beyond, from outside what is governed by the imaginary, by a representation, something which confronts the subject. In this sense the real is by definition only encountered, and by virtue of this fact receives its characteristic structure. As in Proust, the sign of the realness of the real lies in its involuntary nature. It is what is not sought after, the unexpected, predictable only after the fact. Moreover, the real is always some particular encounter, a particular real – in Lacan's use the substantive 'real' can appear not just with the definite article, but with demonstratives and indefinite articles as well. Perhaps the demonstrative or indefinite article more appropriately qualifies the term 'real' contra the rules of grammar than the definite article; the real is essentially not generic but particular. A real is a particular, in Russell's sense.

Milner goes on to equate what is encountered or met with what is *given*. Here, in this term, the empirical as *data*, the 'given', seems to meet the empirical as chance encounter. But the difference between a formulation of the data in terms of what could be imagined as other than it is and the empiricist notion of the data as paradigmatically what is given to observation, understood as sense observation, should not be obscured. The first cannot be reduced to the second; indeed, the definition of the empirical Milner proposes for Koyré's epistemology is carefully formulated so as to avoid the problem of knowledge so typically at the centre of empiricist epistemology and its counterpart in the philosophy of science, the problem of the validation of a scientific knowledge.[36] This is achieved by understanding the given as simply the way things are, with no concern either with how they came to be that way, or with how it can be guaranteed that they are indeed that way. The given thus stands for the set of initial assumptions any science begins with, the things it 'takes as given' and in that sense does not have to establish are given. These are what Chomsky in *Aspects* (pp. 25ff) refers to as 'the primary linguistic data' (see note 48 for reference). The given is encountered by chance in that it is the way it is not out of any necessity.

Without being in every instance separate – for sense-data is a special case of data, if not the only case of it – the empiricalness of the given is by Milner's definition separ*able* from the sensibly observed in a number of ways. Milner provides a crucial example from linguistics: the case of the grammatical categories. Structural linguistics has assumed that its units must be justified preliminary to their being used in the theory, while transformational grammar proceeds as if they are given (p. 89–90) – i.e., it takes them as part of its primary linguistic data. Now if the paradigm case of the grammatical unit is the phoneme, it might plausibly be treated as a sense-datum, though structuralist phonology encountered notorious problems with this assumption, certainly recalling empiricism's attempts to deal with what Russell called 'the gap between the world of physics and the world of sense'. But if we take rather the syntactic units – noun, noun phrase, sentence, and so on – as paradigmatic of what Milner means by the given, their givenness is in no obvious way a matter of being given to the senses. They may never be observed, unless observation is extended to include the mental. If we thus approach the general question of the units from the direction of syntax as opposed to phonology, we can now see how Saussure's classic difficulty with the units – with the necessary segmentation of phonology – clearly turns on the division between the sensibly perceived and the given. Speakers cannot strictly speaking perceive the units via the senses – i.e., instruments cannot record breaks between all units which speakers nonetheless perceive in the sense of encountering them in their knowledge of the language.[37]

That defining the empirical as the contingent is meant to permit the science of linguistics to skirt the whole problem of knowledge centered on sense-perception on the analogy with physics can be surmised from Milner's account of arbitrariness in Saussure, for he claims that 'the arbitrary aims at uprooting linguistics from the verisimilitude of sense impressions', adding: 'One should recall here Koyré's theses on Galilean physics' (p. 95, n. 5). Arbitrariness is then asserted only to name 'the encounter – what Lacan better names contingence, and also what Mallarmé names Chance' (p. 87).

The element of chance in the encounter with the given has negative dimensions as well, which Lacan characterises as 'the encounter in so far as it may be missed, in so far as it is essentially the missed encounter'.[38] Here the non-coincidence of the data with the observed is again apparent, since what is given cannot be observed. At this point, the rationalist definition of the empirical Milner supplies for Koyré can be brought into line with logical empiricism's most celebrated formulation of the demarcation criterion, Popper's notion of falsifiability, which Milner calls 'but an application of condition (2)'[39] specifying that it must be possible to imagine the state of affairs referred to by an empirical statement as different from what it is. But for the falsifiability of the claim made in a scientific proposition to be equated with this formulation of the empirical, falsifiability – a formal condition which the state of affairs referred to by a proposition must meet – cannot be understood to entail falsification, a process which a falsifiable proposition may or may not actually undergo.[40] In this sense, falsifiability, like contingency, is a logical property of some statements and not others, independent of their career in the history of science. It is this property, in part, which sets them off from non-empirical statements.

In other words, a rationalist epistemology of science is not concerned with validity, with setting up guarantees of certitude or even semi-certitude in the area of scientific knowledge; it is concerned only with identifying empirical statements and distinguishing them from those which are not. If the empirical is simply the given, what is encountered by chance, then no methodology can guarantee its discovery ahead of time; it is a particular theory and not methodology which retrospectively reveals the crucial data, those that furnish evidence, those which are susceptible to formalisation: 'it is the result which permits the reorganization and the rethinking of the past. "It is the solution, once found, that reflects its light upon the data" '[41] This applies specifically to the methodological procedures by which the crucial data is found. It is well known that structural linguistics, especially in its American form, heavily influenced by empiricism and behaviourism, conceived of its methodology almost exclusively in terms of the isolation of the data, of 'discovery procedures'. These procedures, moreover, were focused on the problem of determining the units of the language. Attempting to deduce phonemic structural form, the minimal pair test is the obvious case of such a procedure in phonology. Chomsky's rejection of not simply the necessity but the possibility of discovery procedures is hence in keeping with a rationalist epistemology of science.

The negative side of the encounter with the real can be understood in several ways. It can mean that non-observed or even impossible states of affairs can constitute evidence – a kind of negative thought experiment. We recall the first of Milner's conditions for a statement to be empirical: direct or indirect representability in time and space. It should be noted that the state of things referred to need not actually occur in time and space; it must only be so representable. Thus, in Milner's epistemology, the generative grammarian's attention to syntax and its evidence in the form of native speakers' judgements presents no problem in meeting Milner's conditions for empiricalness and the charge of 'mentalism' levelled by structuralists and behaviourists at such evidence is deprived of its validity; this mentalism is not unempirical.

The speaker's judgements are akin to sense-data in their subjectivity. The history of physical science has dealt with this subjective data by externalising it as much as possible from the observer, thereby rendering it impersonal, if subjective; such is the function of the scientific instrument, as well as of rigorous measurement. The image on the lens of the telescope remains subjective in that it exists in subjective time and space – i.e., it is tied to a single perspective – but it is objectivised by not being dependent on a single observer.[42] Such also is the function of the repeated experiment under ideal conditions. In the case of linguistic evidence, the consulting of speakers' judgements is a kind of experiment; the utterance is externalised from one particular speaker and made accessible to the judgement of others. More important, as in physical science, it is the theory which disconnects the evidence from the observer. Consider those cases Chomsky discusses where speakers disagree or are undecided as to the grammatical status of a string of formatives in some language; in such cases, Chomsky argues, the theory must decide – i.e., in favour of the decision which favours the most elegant and least *ad hoc* solution, all other things being equal.

The negative side of the empirical as missed encounter can also be that possible state of affairs that does not obtain but if it did would falsify the empirical claim which asserts its contrary. Not only what turns out 'to be the case' but also whatever is not the case', to echo the opening of Wittgenstein's *Tractatus*,[43] what is not determined by any logical necessity, could thus always be the contrary of the scientist's claim. Not that science is a game of chance, but insofar as the laws of the universe are not legislated by the scientist – indeed, are not legislated at all – science's claims are of the nature of intelligent guesses, as Pascal was aware.[44]

But the missed encounter can also refer to the situation in which the scientist does not encounter a real at all, or not one which can be represented by a general law, the case in which there is no breakthrough and which makes scientific research no guarantee of results.

For if the real which science has to do with is recognisable in its quality of being either simply given, simply there, or not, fomalisable or not, for whoever is so lucky to come upon it, if it does not necessarily yield itself to methodic research but rather makes itself known as what is beyond the control of the scientist's wishes or expectations, then it is no wonder it takes on the features of a love. Each science encounters a real whose features in no way resemble those which are the object of another science, giving rise to formal representations peculiar to it, defining the issues of the science in a way that could not have been predicted by any general methodology.[45] Not, of course, Barthes's notion of 'the impossible science of the unique being',[46] for science, the possible sort, aims at the universal, formulating the laws which predict what is regular, rule-governed, but with this qualification. The features of the real each science encounters may turn out not to be generalisable beyond the domain defined by that real, even when it interacts with the real of another science. Hence the incommunicability of the experience of the encounter in which the real permits representation.

It is at this point that the characteristic formulations of a rationalist epistemology of science join with a familiar theme of French literature. It appears perhaps first in Pascal, post-Galilean mathematician, bearing witness to a common preoccupation of French science and literature. Milner, as we saw, invokes Mallarmé's chance. But it is in Proust especially that a literary search and a scientific research are both seen as dependent on a prior chance encounter with a real that imposes itself with the same arbitrariness as the object of desire, never deliberately chosen, never replaceable by another so long as it imposes itself. Such are the features of the reminiscences Proust seeks to decipher, 'those [truths] which life communicates to us against our will', the real as the involuntary:

> they composed a magical scrawl, complex and elaborately flourished, their essential character was that I was not free to choose them, that such as they were they were given to me. And I realised that this must be the mark of their authenticity. I had not gone in search of the two uneven paving-stones of

the court-yard upon which I had stumbled. But it was precisely the fortuitous and inevitable fashion in which this and the other sensations had been encountered that proved the trueness of the past which they brought back to life, of the images which they released, since we feel, with these sensations, the effort that they make to climb towards the light, feel in ourselves the joy of rediscovering what is real.[47]

LINGUISTICS' ENCOUNTER WITH THE REAL OF LANGUAGE

It is both a strong claim and a central theme of *For the Love of Language* that linguistics, too, has come up against a real, one in language, and has found a way to formalise it. That real is identified at the start: it is the fact that not everything can be said, what Milner calls the 'impossible' in language. It sets a limit to language, differentiating the grammatical from the agrammatical.[48] Moreover, that real is in no way created or legislated by the grammarian; like the truths which Proust stumbles against, it imposes itself on speakers against their will. That this impossibility should have the force of law is not due to the fact that some have set themselves up to legislate it but that, as some have discovered, the limits it sets can be predicted by general rules.

Indeed, the notion of the impossible is linked paradoxically to that of the real. The real is the state of affairs that can be imagined as other than it is because there is no reason why it is the way it is. But it is not other than it is. In this sense, it is impossible for it to be otherwise and continue to be itself. There may be a possible world in which things could have turned out to be different, but once one is in one possible world, its nature is not to be other than it is. This inability of a given world, a given state of affairs, to be other than it is, is what Milner, following Lacan, means by the impossible.

That impossibility, insofar as it defines a contingent state of affairs, is at one and the same time epistemic and deontic; in other words, it is both the case that not everything can be said and that there is a prohibition against saying just anything. In linguistics, these two interpretations of the impossible in language are in general counterposed; one is descriptive and the other normative, and a grammatical theory is assumed to treat its rules as either one or the other but not both. Milner, however, argues that what is impossible in language is also forbidden. The analogy he draws is with the incest taboo, which he characterises likewise as an impossible which is also a prohibition (pp. 105–6). What he means by this is made clearer by his discussion of the notion of a grammatical rule in an article published in the *Encyclopédie Universalis* as 'Grammaire'. In it he writes, 'the grammatical judgement appears to have the form of a value judgement. This is connected to the fact that the impossible of language is in no way a material impossible: a sentence considered teratological by all the speakers of a given language can always, despite this, be produced, even if only in jest. Similarly, speaking subjects can produce every type of form, including those called defective, without running any physical risk' (p. 746). In other words, the impossible in language, as in the incest taboo, is no physical impossibility, and yet it nonetheless exists *in* language. Its effect is not to prevent agrammatical sentences from being produced but to mark them as agrammatical, to distinguish between the correct and the incorrect. 'In that sense', Milner observes, 'if one agrees to consider all distinctions a norm, then all grammar is normative' (p. 747). The peculiar nature of the impossible in language, of its laws and rules, is thus a function of its being non-physical.

For the real of language exists in language and not in the world or even in the relation of language to the world. It is in 'the dimension of the purely grammatical', as Foucault has called it,[49] that linguistics locates its real. This, we shall see shortly, identifies a crucial step in the isolation of the real of language for the history of linguistics. For Milner, it has another consequence as well. With linguistics, the empirical need no longer coincide with the physical: 'the agency of the One thus takes on a new form – from time immemorial, philosophy had recognized it in nature . . . With grammar, and its intersection with science – linguistics – the One appears not only outside of nature, but in the very thing one would have wished to define by this externality. Galileo's small letters are revealed as capable of spelling out something other than the *physis*' (p. 93).

For Milner the existence of linguistics thus precludes the equation of empiricalness with the physical world, and science must now admit what has been classically defined by opposition to the physical and has always stood for the unreal. In view of early generative grammar's response to a behaviouristically oriented structural linguistics' charges of 'mentalism', it might seem that Milner's position is a natural consequence of his generative persuasion. One recalls Chomsky's invocation of Newton's uneasiness with gravity as an 'occult force' as a defence of abstract levels like deep structure. Milner, like Chomsky, is defending the reality of theoretical constructs with no obvious basis in the physical, whether as biology or behaviour. But more recently some generative linguists have attributed to the speaker's 'internalised grammar' a biological reality; it is thus to defend the notion of a real which is not ultimately recuperable by the physical that Milner makes this explicit point. What, then, is at stake in this debate?

The entire argument of *For the Love of Language* is meant to align its author with the realists as opposed to the idealists and nominalists on language. That realism, Milner argues, follows from the epistemology of linguistics, and particularly generative linguistics as the science in question. But Milner makes clear that his philosophical realism in no way entails physicalism.

Milner's position in *For the Love of Language* can be glossed by some brief objections he voiced in another context to the biologism as a form of physicalism espoused by certain generative linguists.[50] The thrust of Milner's argument there is to disconnect the assertion that linguistic theory seeks adequately to represent a reality which exists in language, and hence that its claims are falsifiable, from the further assertions that this reality is (a) psychological and (b) that a psychological reality is a biological state of a mental organ. This disconnection, Milner further argues, actually holds at the level of practice for those who identify themselves as generative linguists, who recognise as possibly falsifying evidence only linguistic evidence as opposed to evidence which is psychological or biological – i.e., non-linguistic.

The issue comes down to Milner's denial that a specific substance must be attributed to what is real. The examples he invokes to demonstrate the non-triviality of the attribution of substance to the real are suggestive. The first is the notion of gravity within Newtonian physics, which we saw Chomsky himself has invoked in the context of a similar debate. As Milner points out in a way familiar within Koyré's epistemology of science, the various positions maintained on the question of the substance of gravity, sometimes by the same individual, in no way prevented success in scientific work on the notion. Milner also invokes Saussure's example of the identity of the 8:45 Geneva-Paris Express, commenting that Saussurean linguistics entertained somewhat sophisticated conceptions of substance. But the example he returns to several times concerns the substance of the incest prohibition. Here it would be rash to conclude that Milner's point is only to connect the real with the structure of the social. The example is meant to invoke Freud, and it is for psychoanalysis that Milner wishes to clear a space for a nonphysical real, one which also in some sense is counterposed to the physical as its 'other'. In so doing, he provides a basis for accepting Lacan's assertion that psychoanalysis is a realism and not an idealism without going so far as Freud to claim it as a science. Desire, then, Freud is understood to argue, is real, but not a real out there in the world; the hysteric is not deluded, but has really though unconsciously desired.[51]

But in insisting on the non-physical nature of the real of language, Milner is not to be understood as identifying linguistics as a humanism. For to claim that linguistics has encountered a real which is formalisable is tantamount to claiming that it is a science in Koyré's sense. The strength of this claim lies in the fact that Milner makes it only of linguistics among the so-called 'human' sciences (p. 78); it does not extend to the others which, according to Milner, 'have typically to do with realities the constraint of which is properly speaking a *parody* of the impossible' (p. 78). Milner's position is thus situated elsewhere than either with the optimistic and extravagant projects of a structuralist poetics or semiotics to construct a science of literature on the model of linguistics, or with the more recent attempts to 'deconstruct' all linguistic theory along with literary theory; linguistics and only linguistics outside the physical sciences can lay claim to being a science. The reason this is so is not explicable in terms of any linguistic methodology, however; it is, Milner insists, attributable only to linguistics' having encountered a real in language susceptible to formalisation.

If this is indeed the case, what consequence does the existence and nature of linguistics as a science have for all those who are concerned with language, both linguists and non-linguists?

GRAMMAR'S TOTALITY VS LINGUISTICS' ALL

Linguistics is not alone in encountering the real in language, but it is alone – so Milner claims – in making from the encounter a science. From the opening pages of *For the Love of Language*, Milner places linguistics alongside other attempts to deal with this real, and the task of defining linguistics as a science is the task of differentiating it from these other loves of language. Foremost among these other approaches to language and the closest to linguistics is grammar. The contrast with grammar is elaborated in part epistemologically and in part historically, parallel to Koyré's treatment of pre-Galilean physics and astronomy in an epistemology of science. Milner treats grammar with the familiarity and respect both of the intellectual tradition which still includes an Académie Française and of that in general evinced by transformational grammar. It is necessary to call attention to this, because in the English-speaking world, where there exists a hatred of language as such, grammar as a discipline has essentially disappeared.[52] To follow Milner's argument, one must have a sense of what he means by grammar.

An encounter with the real separates out both grammar and linguistics from what Milner characterises as 'the various hermeneutic disciplines' (p. 91). From the further decisive meeting of the empirical with the mathematical dates the separation of linguistics from all arts of language, and from it follows all the other differences between grammar and linguistics. The limit between the acceptable and the non-acceptable in the speaker's knowledge of language is discovered to be formally representable as the division between the grammatical and the agrammatical; a limit encountered in the real is embodied in a Galilean writing, and science, in Koyré's sense, is constituted.

The operation by which the formalisable is seized, which is the very experience of science itself, is in Milner's account one of extracting and representing the regularities in the real. This set of regularities Milner calls, after Lacan, a *tout*, that universal quantifier which in French is translatable as either 'all' or 'everything' or as 'whole'. The process of extraction is simultaneously one of exclusion, for not everything in language is formally representable. The all is hence defined by contrast with the not-all, or everything real which escapes formalisation. The initial gesture of science involves then a renunciation – what cannot be rep-

resented by a formal writing is set aside, for there is no necessity
by which all can be mathematicised. Such wilful ignorance is
already in Descartes' project, but it awaits Kant to be made
programmatic.[53] This is classically conceived in structuralist linguistics as the isolation of the object of study. Milner makes clear
what is involved. The object of linguistics is that grammaticality
which is defined by its limits: the existence of the agrammatical.
Linguistics operates on the assumption that this grammaticality
and its limits can be predicted by formal rules; any features not so
representable it will ignore.

Linguistics has given various names both to its object and to
what is excluded from it, to the all and the not-all. The English-
speaking reader is likely to be familiar with Saussure's distinction
between *langue* and *parole*. While it would be a mistake to equate
these notions with Chomsky's notions of competence and
performance, whose content is different, at the level of their
epistemological function they are comparable. Both pairs alike
serve to name the object of study so as to indicate that it is not
all-inclusive. *Langue* and competence then stand for what is
formally representable, *parole* and performance for what is not.[54]
Hence the grab-bag aspect of the latter two notions – e.g., the
typical list of performance errors (see p. 89 of *For the Love of
Language*).

Milner operates with another distinction which we will eventually see is threefold, beginning with a Saussurean opposition
less well known to the English speaker, that between *langue* and
langage. The unfamiliarity of the distinction may be due to the
problem of translating it; unlike *langue* and *parole*, these two
separate items, rendered into English, become indistinguishable. I
have translated them by the distinction between 'language with a
small *l*' and 'Language with a capital *L*'.[55] It is 'language' which
names the object of linguistics; the concept represented by
'Language' belongs to the tradition of non-linguistic, of even
non-grammatical speculation on language, to philosophical grammars, philosophies of Language and treatises on the origin of
Language. Its object does not presumably represent a real. One
might reasonably associate Language with what Foucault describes as 'language . . . defined as discourse', with 'no other
history than that of its representations' and language with what
has 'the dimensions of the purely grammatical'.[56]

In Milner's account, the purely grammatical is already acknowledged in traditional grammar, as opposed to philosophical grammar; but grammar, which is concerned with the rule-governed, does not represent these rules formally. The formal notation is not just a convention, however; its adoption by linguistics alters the conception of grammar's and linguistics' common object, language. The notion of the all linquistics attributes to language is distinct in Milner's account from the unity of language grammar reconstructs. In this he depends upon Lacan's distinction between the imaginary and the symbolic (p. 75), which also allows Milner to identify two different ways of representing the unity formed within the real of language. Grammar's conception of that unity he gives the name 'totality' (p. 75). The meaning he assigns that term derives from the features Lacan associates with the imaginary. Structured by the look, the unity of a totality might be likened to a *Gestalt*. It is seized all at once, 'at a glance'; it is perceivable as a whole. This is what Milner means by saying that grammar constructs an 'image' of language. Moreover, that totalised unity can allow nothing to escape it; there is nothing outside the totality – everything must be completely represented in a grammar. There is no non-totality, as there is a not-all.

The all of linguistics is no imaginary totality. It can be represented only by deliberately ignoring what cannot be formalised. Hence the fragmentary nature of linguistics' account of language, which in no way contradicts the constraints imposed on its theoretical statements – that they account for all and only the sentences of the language. This conception of the whole is indeed contained in the very notion of a symbolic writing. A mathematical writing does not construct an image on a visual or perceptual model; it sets down structures and operations sequentially, accounting only for what can be captured in this writing. The nature of the knowledge thus represented is radically different. No longer presided over by the look, its unit is not containable in a single act of consciousness and hence traceable to an ego, an *I*; it is not graspable all at once but must be set down in the objective form of a mathematical formula.

THE EPISTEMIC BREAK IN THE HISTORY OF LINGUISTICS

The step separating grammar from linguistics is an historical one as well, and Milner's epistemology of linguistics recounts that history *à la* Koyré, locating an 'epistemic break' separating pre-scientific thought from science. For Koyré, the rise of science is tied to the mathematicisation of the empirical as an event in intellectural history. Just as science for Koyré is 'Galilean science' (p. 68) – that is, mathematical or Archimedean physics – and pre-science is Aristotelian or Euclidean physics, either ancient or medieval – or, as the moment of the historical break is approached, one of the various hermeticist or alchemical predecessors of science, its Giordano Bruno as opposed to its Galileo – so linguistics too has its counterparts of science and pre-science, developed, however, in the terms peculiar to its object.

For Milner, the decisive moment marking the break between grammar and linguistics is located in the rise of the comparative grammar of the Indo-European languages. In this, Milner is in agreement with Foucault, both providing an important corrective to the view current outside linguistics that linguistic science begins with Saussurean structuralism (pp. 82–3).[57] But while Foucault sees the crucial change in the shift from language as a system of representations[58] to language as an object, as the purely grammatical, Milner credits traditional grammar, as opposed to the philosophical grammars Foucault treats, with an encounter with the purely grammatical, and sees the crucial departure for comparative grammar in its construction of a formal writing, even if a not fully developed one (p. 94).

The history of this new science after its inception in comparative grammar is understood by Milner in terms of two competing versions of science – two 'ideal sciences' both bespeaking a shared 'ideal of science' which makes it legitimate to speak in the singular of *the* science of linguistics. Milner's account of that history, like any history of science, begins with the recognition of a fact: the former dominance of structuralism and its displacement by generative grammar (p. 81). These two versions of science are identified with partial reference to Koyré, as Aristotelian science, essentially Euclidean, for structuralism, and Galilean or Archimedean science, for transformational grammar. In this history, Saussure occupies a place quite other than the one that structuralism as a general project of the human sciences assigned him. In a history of linguistics which begins with comparative grammar, structuralism becomes a throwback to an earlier position. Such is also the case in Foucault's account of linguistics in the nineteenth century, but with an important difference. For Foucault, Saussure's 'backwardness' is bound to his theory of the sign: 'It was also necessary that Saussure, rediscovering the project of a general semiology, should have given the sign a definition that could seem "psychologistic" (the linking of a concept and an image): this is because he was in fact rediscovering the classical condition for conceiving of the binary nature of the sign' (*The Order of Things*, p. 67). According to Foucault, in the wake of the radical break comparative grammar represented,'Saussure had to by-pass this moment in the history of the spoken word, which was a major event for the whole of nineteenth-century philology, in order to restore, beyond its historical forms, the dimension of language in general, and to reopen, after such neglect, the old problem of the sign, which had continued to animate the whole of thought from Port-Royal to the last of the "Idéologues" ' (p. 286). For Milner, however, Saussure did not provide a theory of the sign at all, neither a classical one nor a new one. Milner treats Saussure not as the originator of a new science but as himself a kind of epistemologist of linguistics, commenting on a pre-existent practice: 'for him, linguistics already existed, namely comparative grammar' (p. 82); 'the object of Saussurean theory is linguistics itself' (p. 86). Saussure's *Course* is thus an attempt to formulate the practising linguist's assumptions in Kantian terms, as the neo-grammarians had done before him.

In the comparison between two models of a science of linguistics, it is the so-called Saussurean theory of the sign that Milner dismantles, what for so many who are outside linguistics constitutes the science of linguistics to the point that linguistics is taken as synonymous with the theory of the sign. Here Milner's logical economy, measuring the Saussurean epistemology of linguistics against another newer but now existing linguistics – transformational grammar – applies Occam's razor explicitly as Chomskyan theory had done in effect to Saussure's putative theory of the sign, exposing in the process the minimal core of a linguistic theory and paring away what is unnecessary. It is the sign itself that is eliminated, its properties now redistributed in generative grammar to other points of the theory.

So contrary to the current orthodoxy outside linguistics is this attack on the sign, and such is the ignorance as to what linguistics is really about that one anonymous reviewer of *For the Love of Language* for an American university press could assert, out of total incomprehension, that Milner had added nothing new to the theory of the sign. Moreover, in the properties assigned the Saussurean sign, Milner finds a significance that runs counter to the facile slogans the general movement called 'structuralism' took from Saussure. This is most apparent with respect to the arbitrariness of the sign, which Milner connects to a number of linguistics' initial assumptions rendering possible the isolation of language as such. The arbitrariness of the sign marks the relation between language and the world (reference), between sound and meaning, as simply a chance encounter. Whatever regularities exist in language (and it is the rule-governed that linguistics is interested in), the account of them cannot go beyond the givens of this encounter, cannot seek for causes to explain why these regularities have the form they do. Thus, in Chomsky, 'explanatory adequacy' is never conceived of in terms of explanatory causes located beyond the grammar, ones invoking meaning, for example, or function or language use (see *Aspects*, pp. 30–7). Rather, explanatory adequacy consists only in providing 'a principled basis for selecting a descriptively adequate grammar on the basis of primary linguistic data by the use of a well-defined evaluation measure' (*Aspects*, p. 34), in other words, 'a way of evaluating alternative proposed grammars' (*Aspects*, p. 31). The only further stipulation that Chomsky makes is that there must be a way of guaranteeing that the most highly valued grammar is sufficiently rich in structure so as to restrict the range of possible hypotheses. Explanatory adequacy thus spells out an epistemological position which assumes the limits of linguistics and the principled decision not to know.

The notion of arbitrariness says nothing about the existence or non-existence of the real.[59] It says only that there are two orders – that of language and that of the world – and that the real *in* language – the grammatical and the agrammatical – is in no way caused by and explicable in terms of any reality outside language (p. 87). Hence, the assertion of the arbitrariness of the sign indicates what it is that linguistics can have nothing to say about: why language is the way it is. It is only the given form of language's existence – one out of a set of possible forms – which is its object; herein lies the nature of its empiricalness. Milner's interpretation of arbitrariness also explicitly rules out conventionalism (n. 11, p. 96), and, a *fortiori*, the whole project of a semiology whereby the form of language is made to follow from a system of conventions and their functions. The same can be said of any functionalist explanation which goes beyond language to any social purposes it may have – for instance, a communications model of language.

LINGUISTICS' RELATION TO *LALANGUE*, THE NOT-ALL OF LANGUAGE

The very possibility of a linguistic science is dependent, then, on this initial gesture by which linguists set aside certain questions as irrelevant to their concerns and represent their object within well-defined limits and subject to well-defined constraints. That object, then, the language of linguistics, is not synonymous with the totalised image of language constructed by grammar or with the Language of philosophy. Its unity, as we have seen, is a fragmentary one, gained by renouncing the goal of representing all; it thereby acknowledges that there is something which escapes it. For the members of Milner's pair language/Language situate themselves not just with respect to one another but with respect to a third term, one coined by Lacan, and which I do not translate: *lalangue*.[60]

Once more, this term is defined by contrast with the other terms it co-occurs with. *Lalangue* is the name of the real in language; it is thus what escapes linguistic theory: the not-all. Indeed, the series *the real, the not-all,* and *lalangue* each occur in a triad, and, returning to the distinctions (pp. 25–7), one can identify a correspondence between Lacan's imaginary, symbolic and real and Milner's particularisation of this triad for language which puts together Saussure and Lacan: Language with a capital *L* corresponds to the imaginary representation; language with a small *l* to the symbolic representation, and *lalangue* to the real. The imaginary Language constitutes a totality; the symbolic language an all or whole, and *lalangue* the not-all. It is in this sense that the imaginary totality can be said to mask the real, to convert it into something seemingly explicable; its representation gives no sign of incompleteness. Having no formal constraints on that representation, it manages to give some explanation of everything. If the real in Lacan's formula is what escapes representation, its existence is nonetheless not denied by the whole or all constructed out of linguistics' formal writing; it is rather deliberately ignored. Linguists are not unaware of the existence of those things in language which interest psychoanalysis: slips of the tongue, plays on words, and so on. These they would not construe as having no status as real. On the contrary, the homophony they bear witness to in language – the accidental falling together of sounds and constructions – is in no way imaginary. Only, despite its realness, linguists must ignore homophony as the precondition of their science. Real, yet unlike the real of the agrammatical, it is resistant to formal representation.

Yet out of the real, Milner insists, linguistics has extracted an all which it symbolically represents. This relation between symbolic and real is finally the subject of *For the Love of Language*. It is at the ever-shifting yet nonetheless clearly demarcated boundaries between the two that linguists find themselves; there they yield to their desire. But it would be to miss the whole point of Milner's own subtle reading of Lacan to draw as the predictable conclusion to this confrontation between linguist and the object of the linguist's desire the impossibility of representing that real and the fictional status of the linguist's representations. For it *is* written, and that, not by virtue of anything the linguist, as opposed to the social scientist, for instance, has done, but by virtue of something in language, by virtue of the formalisable nature of some real in it. That in that real there should be something that can be represented by a writing is in *For the Love of Language* the fundamental state of affairs rendering both linguistics and the linguist's experience of science possible, while at the same time in no way an expected or predictable state of affairs. The non-necessary and hence startling aspect of this state of affairs Milner never ceases to stress; it is what no logic could have predicted (p. 67). It is moreover what the current dismissal of linguistics wishes to deny, and in so denying it, the linguist is deprived of any other than an illusory object of desire (p. 62–3). Herein lies the crucial role of Milner's psychoanalysis of the experience of science. For whosoever has had this experience, the features of that all delineated against the backdrop of the not-all are unmistakably revealed in a form for which there exists an adequate mathematical representation. For the interval, something ceases to not be written. It is this which is at the heart of the linguist's love. For it is a *love* of language which endows the linguist's enterprise with its special character, and not simply a desire. If for Lacan, there is no sexual relation, the union of the sexes is an impossible one, desire being the form of that impossibility, an impossibility which, according to the formula of *Encore*, 'does not cease to not be written', it should not escape notice that in that seminar Lacan introduces another, quite distinct term, 'love'. Love, according to Lacan, negates the impossibility contained in what does not cease to not be written; instead, it never ceases to be written.[61]

It is not simply philology – that name generally assigned the appearance of linguistics in the nineteenth century – which suggests Milner's title. Milner's choice of this one term 'love' among other possibilities is meant accurately to identify the linguistic enterprise, even the unpoetic and tedious academic writing which sets down the arguments the linguist finds for it. By virtue of this love, unlike the often empty meanderings of the various hermeneutic disciplines or the forced optimism of the social sciences, linguistics is never sad, that adjective which in French suggests the pathetic, the depressing. For linguistics has its thrill peculiar to it. That every true linguist knows, and if it cannot be transmitted directly to another, it can be read, can be reactivated, for those who are able and persistent enough to decipher it, in the formal intricacies of linguistic argumentation, whenever they sucessfully touch the real, whenever *lalangue* yields to the linguist a glimpse of the knowledge of language.

THE LINGUIST'S RELATION TO LALANGUE: SAUSSURE, JAKOBSON, CHOMSKY

In the series of existential statements which mark the stages of Milner's argument and characterise his style, the existence of the linguist's thrill – a kind of Lichtenbergian *cogitatur*: '*lalangue* knows' or 'there is some all extractable from *lalangue*' – forms the grounds of a certainty for linguistics. This is perhaps why Milner can conclude: 'Such is indeed the uncertainty which guides linguists, as long as the real import of psychoanalysis remains unknown to them' (p. 67). For this reason, to any epistemology of science, even if depsychologised, must be added a psychoanalysis of scientific knowledge. Nor is it surprising that Lacan, in attaching Freud to a philosophical tradition, should do so via the notion of the subject. But in Lacan's concept of the 'subject of the unconscious,' the Cartesian *cogito* is detached from consciousness and shorn of the ego in which subjectivity – the subjectivity that furnishes the grounds for certainty – is now shown not to reside.

For the linguist, the thrill lies at that point where evidence meets theory; this is the point where the all emerges in its mathematicisable form out of the not-all, where *lalangue*, as opposed to either linguist or speaker, knows. For this reason, far from operating in involuntary ignorance of *lalangue*, of those of its features consigned to the not-all, the linguist, as much as anyone concerned with language, as much as the poet or the literary critic, must constantly confront what it is that escapes formalisation. If, as Milner points out, the linguist's ignorance of the not-all is wilful, a principled decision to ignore, to not know (p. 60) which structures linguistics (p. 74) – in Saussure this refusal of knowledge being directed toward what is labelled the arbitrary – then the experience of science the linguist is granted involves a relation, albeit negative, to the not-all, to *lalangue*, this other of the 'language' of linguistics. And the will not to know all must be constantly exerted in the face of a return of the not-all. This negative relation is the other side of that encounter with the real which is the subject of *For the Love of Language*. Since it structures a private experience, its particular form varies with the individual linguist, constitutes a biography, appropriately understood through a psychoanalysis of the knowledge which it causes to be written, to cease to not be written. For these individual experiences give shape to the body of knowledge that is written in formal symbols. That knowledge is objective, in that, as science, the structure realised by the writing of linguistics it comes to have is independent of the linguist's will; it is subjective insofar as it emerges out of that experience in which the real is seized and formalised.

The history of linguistic science which follows thus presents a series of representatives of that science who are also decked out in the guise of lovers of language, and it is as much the way they deal with the not-all as the form they give to the all which distinguishes them. Milner's representative linguists are Saussure, Jakobson, and Chomsky (though others are supplied), the contrast between Saussure and Chomsky operating in *For the Love of Language* and that between Saussure and Jakobson elsewhere.[62] They stand for the stages of linguistics' integration into science. But in this guise, they reveal a further truth – that no one is the master of language, that its laws are given by no law-giver. And, as lovers of a language which yields its knowledge not by the imposition of the linguist's will but via the fortuitous encounter, they find themselves not in the position of masters but of servants – like all lovers, cutting absurd and even ridiculous figures, but ultimately redeemed only by the results of their endeavours. It is in this sense that, as Milner puts it, linguistics importunes. For it has, he claims, like Freud's Copernican revolution, dealt a blow to man's narcissism, displacing him from the centre of his language (p. 137).

The measure of linguistics' ability to disturb the man-centred concept of language can be read in the story of Saussure's mad pursuit of the anagrams. For Saussure himself, having recognised that language knows, is the first to be disturbed by it. It is not that the juxtaposition of phonemes Saussure discovers in Saturnian poetry does not exist in language – they have as undeniably occurred as slips of the tongue – it is that he must ascribe to this accidental falling together of elements of sound a conscious intentionality, a legislator, thereby undoing the arbitrariness of the sign. Here Saussure, the subject of that experience of a science of language which is comparative grammar, finds the implications of the knowledge it contains unbearable. Milner finds an analogy for Saussure and the anagrams from the history of science in Cantor's finding in set theory a divine intention (p. 115). Jakobson, by contrast with Saussure, presents another way of dealing with this new knowledge of language, one with its counterpart as well in the history of science. In an obituary dedicated to Jakobson entitled 'Renaissance et Jakobson', meant perhaps to recall Jakobson's obituary for Majakovskij (p. 142),[62] Milner describes Jakobson's characteristic way of incorporating the propositions of a new science – some his own contribution – into another, pre-Galilean way of thinking. Jakobson, Milner tells us, when he spoke French, never said *langue* – language – but always *langage* – Language. To Saussure's distinction he preferred a maxim adapted from Terence: 'Nil linguistici a me alienum puto'. Jakobson's object was a totality without limits. 'There is nothing foreign to my object – how singular a maxim in the light of our epistemological traditions, which, in fact, strongly maintain science to be defined by its having boundaries and its object by having limits', Milner comments (p. 62). Moreover, for Jakobson, science is reduced to the search for symmetries.

Milner also finds a counterpart for Jakobson in the history of science:

> A reliable witness reports a conversation in which Jakobson marvelled that the metrical formula which he himself had recognised in some Japanese verses repeated the formula of physics recognised by the latest Nobel laureate – who was Japanese – in some atomic structure. His interlocutor on that occasion, most likely formed in the school of Koyré, expressed a limited enthusiasm. Perhaps he had even murmured – supposing him to be a Spinozist – 'man is not an empire within an empire; henceforth it is vain to imagine a human production repeats, as the little repeats the big, a configuration discovered by physics'. His interlocutor, no doubt, had good arguments, and yet he had missed something: he was not able to recognise a claim which had come from elsewhere, from before Galileo, inserting itself, like a *hapax*, into the straight line of scientific discourse. Jakobson was indeed speaking of science, and any person who should happen to hear him was right to understand by science what had gone by that name since Galileo; nevertheless, via a homonymy and a studied Amphibology, it was permissible to understand something else – the science of John Dee, of Giordano Bruno, of Hermes Trismegistus.
>
> He who wished to be a stranger to nothing was thus revealed to be the Stranger *par excellence*. In a universe marked by the Counter-Renaissance, he revived the forgotten figure: the learned doctor, master of the macrocosm and microcosm, doctor of intelligible and material forms, teacher of their harmonies. Like Dee and Bruno, constant journeying formed him, a journeying amidst flames and ruins. Even the places match: Prague, the city of hermeticists, was the place that received the new Magus of the West (pp. 64–5).

Thus Jakobson, in Milner's account, is 'a return to what had preceded' the 'Counter-Renaissance', a term Milner here borrows from Gouhier to designate the post-Galilean period. The role of reconsituter of an older tradition, we have seen, is reserved by Foucault for Saussure. Foucault is right to point out how antithetical a theory of the sign is to what is essential in the new linguistic concept of language. But Milner, it will be remembered, rescues

Saussure's *use* of the sign for a general linguistics (as opposed to a general grammar) from what has traditionally been included in a *theory* of the sign. It is Saussure's interpreters who represent a throwback to an earlier way of thinking. Saussure himself in Milner's account presents the tragic figure of one driven mad by a knowledge which he sees all too clearly but which he is unable to render anodyne, consoling, useful. The contrast with Milner's portrait of Jakobson is all too clear:

> the subject who believed in symmetries knew how to regulate his own destiny in terms of them. And yet, might it be permitted for a modern to take from this accomplishment the indication of a weakness? How can one completely believe in this universe unrent, unlacerated, how can one believe that symmetry and asymmetry will suffice entirely to fill in the gaps? How can one not oppose to the happy figure of Jakobson the shattered figure of Saussure? The latter, an aristocrat, rich, handsome, living in a chateau, in a country at peace, never knew rest. At the very heart of Science, he had stumbled against the stone of scandal, and, as far as one can judge, never recovered from it. The former, a commoner, a Jew, poor, wandering through wars and revolutions, established over all things the reign of symmetry. Encountering himself the fatal anagram, he even succeeded in absorbing from it the effect of radical symmetry. Such success cannot satisfy. We take it as the greatest strangeness of all today: an ethics of happiness which is an ethics of symmetry, wrung from losses and abandonments (p. 66).

It is only with Chomsky that linguistics is fully integrated into Galilean science. What follows, in Milner's account, is Chomsky's politics – not, as others have argued, a set of ideological positions which are the direct logical result of Chomsky's theory of language and mind but as the compensation for a theory of language which deprives man of his full freedom as subject in language.

But if, from the point of view of the history of science, linguists are now firmly established members of what is called 'the academy of science', the special nature of the object of their new science serves only to increase their isolation; 'the impossible in it never ceases to be misunderstood' (pp. 77–8). If they behave like scientists, it is still with those other than linguists concerned with language and not with other scientists that they must continue to carry on the greater part of their intellectual exchange outside linguistics itself. And the full accession of linguistics to science accomplished with Chomsky has only widened the gulf that separates them from these non-linguists. It is the latter who are currently among those who find linguistics' claims the most importunate, who continuously fail to understand the impossible in language, who have had no experience of science, and hence no certainty that the real exists in language and that some part of it is formalisable, who deny the legitimacy of linguistics' renunciation to know all and hence dispute the scientificity of any study of language, given the evidence of *lalangue*. But if indeed linguistics as Milner describes it does exist, and, *a fortiori*, the language it takes as its object, all the pronouncements on death and obsolescence are to no avail in changing the real status and shape of language itself, and its effects for speakers. The exploration of only some of these have been undertaken. What is required is not the construction of other sciences on the linguistic model, for these attempts have not demonstrated that they have encountered any formalisable real. Rather, the actual findings of linguistics must be seriously taken into account by those who hope – or hoped – to find in language some truth.

Fifteen years ago, Foucault undertook such a project in *The Order of Things*. He concludes his account of linguistics in the nineteenth century, treating it together with the political economy of labour and the biology of life, by listing what he calls 'three compensations' for the 'demotion of language to the mere status of object' (p. 296). The first is the development of a symbolic logic and the second is that of 'all the techniques of exegesis' (pp. 297–8). 'Thus the methods of interpretation of modern thought are opposed by the techniques of formalization' (p. 298) – what he calls 'the nineteenth century's double advance, on the one hand towards formalism in thought and on the other towards the discovery of the unconscious – towards Russell and Freud' (p. 299). These two 'compensations' for the blow dealt man's narcissism by linguistics strangely meet in *For the Love of Language* – symbolic logic transcribing the content of the linguist's encounter with the real in language and psychoanalysis interpreting the linguist's experience of that encounter. But it is the third and last compensation Foucault calls 'the most important, and also the most unexpected' – 'the appearance of literature, of literature as such' (p. 299). Literature as such, appearing in the same century as comparative grammar, Foucault defines as 'the isolation of a particular language whose peculiar mode of being is "literary" . . . existing wholly in reference to the pure act of writing' (p. 300). 'Literature', Foucault asserts, 'is the contestation of philology (of which it is nevertheless the twin figure)': 'At the moment when language, as spoken and scattered words, becomes an object of knowledge, we see it reappearing in a strictly opposite modality: a silent, cautious deposition of the word upon the whiteness of a piece of paper, where it can possess neither sound nor interlocutor, where it has nothing to say but itself, nothing to do but shine in the brightness of its being' (p. 300). Deleuze more recently observes apropos of this text: 'What is curious is that Foucault here gives to language, in his beautiful analysis of modern literature, a privilege that he refuses to life and labor' (*Foucault*, p. 139). The privileging of language was once on the agenda. But the slogans derived from linguistics' treatment of it – the arbitrariness of the sign, its conventional origins, the non-referentiality of language – can plausibly be seen not as truths testified to by linguistics, but as attempts to reinstate man as speaker and subject within language, and thereby to restore to him an imaginary mastery over it. It may be that that mastery for some, in the final twist, only makes man the ultimate artificer in a universe of his own making, in which there is no real but only fictions. Yet, beneath the tireless volubility producing our current fictions, the lovers of language can be heard to murmur, like Galileo, for whoever should care to listen, 'but still it speaks, but still it knows, still language sets the limits to what can be said and not be said'.

Notes

1. Cf. also, for example, Chomsky's name mentioned in Woody Allen's *Manhattan* and in his *New Yorker* short story 'The Whore of Mensa' or in Norman Mailer's *The Armies of the Night*.
2. Marcel Proust, *Cities of the Plain*, C. K. Scott Moncrieff (trans.) (New York: Random House, 1927/1955) pp. 248–9.
3. See, for instance, Ian Robinson's *The New Grammarian's Funeral* (Cambridge: Cambridge University Press, 1975), Claude Hagège's *La Grammaire Générative: Réflexions Critiques* (Paris: PUF, 1976), and Geoffrey Sampson's *Making Sense* (Oxford: Oxford University Press, 1980). The hysterical edge of many of these pronouncements as to the

death of linguistics, particularly of generative grammar, is striking. The jacket of Sampson's book, for example, comments: '*Making Sense* shows the discipline of "theoretical linguistics" as a self-created, self-governing, self-directed, self-justifying – though possibly unconscious – academic hoax. In simple language it shows how modern linguists have dressed up unsurprising observations with complex structural paraphernalia and pseudo-scientific gobbledegook. It will be read with pleasure by all who fear that man's humanity is threatened by the importunate advances of an over-acquisitive "scientism" '. Without judging a book by its cover, one cannot help but think, in the face of such statements, of what Milner says of linguistics' threat to man's narcissism (see my Introduction, pp. 34–5). For linguistics does importune, and not the least of the ways it does is in the difficulty of its content.

4. I am inspired here by the only apparent redundancy of the course title, 'English as a Language', used by Julian Boyd at the University of California, Berkeley.

5. Roland Barthes, *The Pleasure of the Text*, Richard Howard (trans.) (New York: Hill & Wang, 1975) pp. 25–6.

6. Gilles Deleuze, *Proust and Signs*, Richard Howard (trans.) (New York: Braziler, 1972) pp. 149 and 145. See also Jacques Lacan, *Le Seminaire Livre XX: Encore* (Paris: Seuil, 1975) p. 26: 'the bee transporting the pollen from the male flower to the female flower – this is what greatly resembles what is involved in communication' (p. 26).

7. As an editor of the *Cahiers Pour l'Analyse*, the journal of the Epistemological Circle of the Ecole Normale Supérieure, Milner contributed toward making Lacan known to a wider audience.

Milner was one of several French-speaking linguists–Nicolas Ruwet was another–brought to MIT in the mid-1960s through the mediation of Roman Jakobson. When, in the wake of May 1968, generative linguistics in Paris could establish itself at the university, at Vincennes (Paris VIII) and elsewhere – independent of the structuralist Martinet at the Sorbonne – Paris became in the next two decades an important and productive centre of 'generativists', as generative grammarians are called in France, gathering together such linguists as François Dell, Pierre Encrevé, Gilles Fauconnier, Hélène Huot, Pierre Pica, Mitsou Ronat, Alain Rouveret, Nicolas Ruwet, Jean-Roger Vergnaud, the Americans Richard Carter, Jacqueline Guéron, and Richard Kayne, and visitors like Joseph Emonds, Morris Halle, S.-Y. Kuroda, Tanya Rinehard, Luigi Rizzi and Sanford Schane.

8. *De l'Ecole* (Paris: Seuil, 1984), Milner's discussion of education in France, which was the object of so much attention and controversy in the year or so after its publication, appears to occupy a separate position. In a fuller discussion of Milner's work, however, it could be placed with respect to the other titles mentioned. As for any relation with *For the Love of Language*, it is perhaps natural that Milner's reflections in the latter on the factors tying the linguist, unlike other scientists, to the school (pp. 129ff.) should then direct attention to the school itself.

9. In other words, a figure who is not the subject of science. Here we can place Milner's hostility to the universal teacher in *De l'Ecole*: 'Thus, whenever one wishes to describe any particular educational content, one always arrives at an *at the same time*: a subject who is healthy of body and at the same time of mind, intelligent and at the same time of heartfelt generosity, amorous, passionate and at the same time an attentive spouse, modest and at the same time brilliant, and in addition, clever with the hands, and so on; this is the result that every true educator must aim for, in short, the total man, of which the French *cavalier* and the English gentleman of the past and the unionized teacher, do-it-yourselfer and athlete of today, are respective illustrations' (p. 57).

10. Bertrand Russell, *Mysticism and Logic* (Garden City, N.Y.: Doubleday, 1957) p. 17.

11. Russell, 'The Philosophy of Logical Atomism,' in *Logic and Knowledge* (New York: Macmillan, 1956) p. 178.

12. 'The impression is for the writer what experiment is for the scientist, with the difference that in the scientist the work of the intelligence precedes the experiment and in the writer it comes after the impression'. *The Past Recaptured*, Andreas Mayor (trans.) (New York: Random House, 1971) p. 140. For Alexandre Koyré, the theory comes before – what he calls the 'primacy of the theory over the facts'. *Etudes d'Histoire de la Pensée Scientifique* (Paris: PUF, 1966) p. 69 – but methodology follows, if not at the very end, at least after the elaboration of the former: 'I consider the place of methodology not to be at the beginning of scientific development, but so to speak in its middle'. *Etudes d'Histoire de la Pensée Scientifique*, p. 64. See also Deleuze, *Proust and Signs*, pp. 94 and 151.

13. Chomsky, in his early polemics against structural linguistics, criticised the latter's preoccupation with necessarily prior 'discovery procedures'. Koyré makes the distinction between 'methods' and 'methodology'. *Etudes d'Histoire de la Pensée Scientifique*, p. 69.

14. There is an important place for introductory texts within linguistics. But outside linguistics, the period of interest in linguistics gave rise to the phenomenon of an intellectual generation many of whom relied for their understanding of linguistics on commentaries written by non-linguists – Jonathan Culler's *Structuralist Poetics* (Ithaca, N.Y.: Cornell University Press, 1975) for instance.

15. 'Yet all the same, it is intellect we must call on to establish this inferiority [of the intellect]. Because if intellect does not deserve the crown of crowns, only intellect is able to award it. And if intellect only ranks second in the hierarchy of virtues, intellect alone is able to proclaim that the first place must be given to instinct'. *Contre Sainte-Beuve* in *Proust on Art and Literature*? S. T. W. (trans.) (New York: Meridian Books, Chatto & Windus, 1958) pp. 25–6.

16. *The Pleasure of the Text*, p. 63.

17. J.-C. Milner, *Les Noms Indistincts* (Paris: Seuil, 1973) p. 48. To be exact, Milner here speaks of a hatred of *lalangue*, a notion which we have yet to discuss. In Milner's text, that hatred is introduced in the context of

a discussion of English as the contemporary candidate for the ideal language. If what is new in the current notion of the ideal language, according to Milner, is the fact that it is presented as what will dispense with all language, it is symptomatic, he adds, that it should be English out of all languages which has appropriated this function, for it is the disappearing language *par excellence*, whose end is marked by Joyce as by the *talkies* and *journalese* (p. 47), here echoing Borges's claim that it is English which is presently the most endangered language precisely because it is the most universal. Might we not also see English as the object *par excellence* of that hatred – not mainly on the part of the subject peoples made to speak it, Joyce included, but on the part of those who speak it natively, imposing it on others, and the English-speaking world of today, intolerant of bilingualism or history of the language, with no grammar schools or dadaists, as the purest realisation of that 'modern world' whose 'dismal secret' Milner equates with the very hatred of language by contrast with systems of communication? Milner's apologia is thus directed not only at the bored but at those who hate language *per se*, whether English or French.

18. This is the same seminar whose 19 December 1972 session is dedicated to Jakobson, then in Paris to deliver his lectures at the Collège de France.

19. In the text of Seminar XX, Lacan introduces Milner by saying that 'no one is more qualified to speak on the position of the linguist' (p. 92).

20. *Encore*, pp. 92–3.

21. *Feminine Sexuality*, Juliet Mitchell and Jacqueline Rose (trans.) (New York: W. W. Norton, 1982).

22. The phrase is the subtitle of Gaston Bachelard's *La Formation de L'Esprit Scientifique: Contribution à une Psychanalyse de la Connaissance Objective* (Paris: Vrin, 1938, 1986).

23. This is not to say that the word 'epistemology' does not appear in English usage with the meaning in question it has in French. 'Epistemology', as it is used by Popper in the Preface to the 1959 English edition of *The Logic of Scientific Discovery* (New York, Harper & Row, 1959), refers first of all to a general theory of knowledge or what Popper here calls 'the growth of knowledge'. It is only within the context of this assumption that Popper can make the specific claim: '*the growth of knowledge can be studied best by studying the growth of scientific knowlege*' (p. 15, Popper's emphasis); in other words, the epistemologist is ideally a philosopher of science, but is not that by definition. When the words 'epistemology' and 'epistemologist' have that definition, they seem often to be translations from their cognates in some other language, as in Einstein's phrase 'the systematic epistemologist' cited in P. Feyerabend, *Problems of Empiricism: Philosophical Papers II*, (Cambridge: Cambridge University Press, 1981), p. 198, n. 58, or in Feyerabend's own text. Another example occurs in the English translation of Gilles Deleuze's *Cinema I: The Movement-Image*: 'we recall Bergson's profound desire to produce a

philosophy which would be that of modern science (not in the sense of a reflection on that science, that is an epistemology)' (Minneapolis: University of Minnesota Press, 1986) p. 60. All these examples constitute exceptions that prove the rule.

24. Bachelard may be known to some in the English-speaking world as an epistemologist of science by way of his influence on Althusser. More typically, however, Bachelard's reputation in English is tied to his later work within 'poetics', and the introduction by Northrop Frye to *The Psychoanalysis of Fire* in 1964, the first translation of a work of Bachelard's into English, effectively associates him with literary criticism in the mind of an English and American public. Other similar works have appeared in English since 1964 – *The Poetics of Space* in 1969, *The Poetics of Reverie* in 1971,*Water and Dreams* in 1983 – but it was not until 1985 that one of Bachelard's many works on epistemology appeared in English, *The New Scientific Spirit*, thus reversing the chronology of his reputation in French. (This one-sided view of Bachelard's work is not present in C. G. Christofides's original essay introducing Bachelard in English, which discusses the epistemological work as well. See 'Bachelard's Aesthetics', *JAAC*, XX, 3, 1962.) Koyré's reputation in English is more firmly established; indeed, Koyré lectured at Johns Hopkins in the 1950s and published certain of his works originally in English. But it still remains the case that his role in the study of the history and philosophy of science, while certainly influential in English, has been less acknowledged (see n. 27 below).

25. The notion of an epistemic break Foucault takes from Bachelard; Koyré presents his own version of the break. It is from Koyré that Foucault takes the term *episteme*, which for Koyré, according to Milner, meant 'the *ancient* conception of science as opposed to modern science' while for Foucault 'it designates the system of production of informative and meaningful statements that is characteristic of a certain discourse configuration' ('Lacan and the Ideal of Science', forthcoming), thus expanding it to encompass any historically characterisable unit of knowledge as part of a larger epistemological project not limited to the sciences which he calls an 'archaeology' of knowledge.

See also the references to the notion of an epistemological break appearing in Lacan's *Ecrits*, listed in the 'classified index of major concepts' in Alan Sheridan's translation of the *Ecrits* (New York; W. W. Norton, 1977) p. 331. The connection made there between epistemology and the 'theory of ideology' is one drawn by Sheridan, and particularly English.

26. Cf. 'There has been much discussion of the role of observation and experiment, of the birth of an "experimental attitude". It is certainly true that the experimental character of classical science is one of its most typical features. In fact, however, it is easy to misundersand just what is involved here. The only role in the birth of classical physics played by observation, in the sense of *simple* observation, the

observation of common sense, was that of an obstacle. The physics of the Parisian nominalists – even that of Aristotle – was often much more akin to such observation than was that of Galileo. As for experimentation – the methodical interrogation of nature – it presupposes both the language in which its questions are to be posed and a terminology which makes it possible to interpret nature's replies. But if it is in a mathematical (or more precisely, geometrical) language that nature is interrogated by classical physics, then this language, or to put it more accurately, the decision to use it – a decision which corresponds to a change of metaphysical attitude – cannot itself be the product of the experiment which is conditioned by it' A. Koyré, *Galileo Studies*, John Mepham (trans.) (New Jersey: Humanities Press, 1978) p. 2.

Or again: 'the manner in which Galileo conceives a correct scientific method involves a predominance of reason over simple experience, the substitution of ideal models (mathematics) for an empirically known reality, the primacy of theory over facts. It is only in this way that the limits of Aristotelian empiricism could be overcome and that a true *experimental* method could be elaborated, a method in which mathematical theory determines the very structure of experimental research, or, to take up again Galileo's own terms, a method which utilizes mathematical (geometric) language in order to formulate its questionings of nature and to interpret nature's answers, one which, substituting the rational Universe of precision for the approximate world known empirically, adopts measurement as a fundamental experimental principle and the most important one. It is this method which, founded on the mathematicization of nature, was conceived and developed, if not by Galileo himself, whose experimental work is practically without value, and who owes his reputation as an experimenter to the indefatigable methods of positivist historians, at least by his disciples and his successors. As a consequence, Mr. Crombie seems to me to exaggerate somewhat the "experimental" aspect of the science of Galileo and the closeness of its links with the achievements of experiment – in fact, Galileo is wrong every time he confines himself to experience'. *Etudes d'Histoires de la Pensée Scientifique*, p. 69.

Or again: 'Before the advent of Galilean science, we accepted with more or less adjustment and interpretation, no doubt, the world given to our senses as the real world. With Galileo and after him, we have a rupture between the world given to the senses and the real world, that of science'. *Etudes d'Histoire de la Pensée Scientifique*, p. 47.

27. Kuhn's acknowledgement of Koyré's influence is curiously vague. In his introduction to *The Structure of Scientific Revolutions*, sketching the background of what he characterises as 'the historiographic revolution in the study of science', Kuhn pronounces this new historiography 'perhaps best exemplified in the writings of Alexandre Koyré' (Chicago: Chicago University Press, 1962) p. 3. But thereafter there is not a single reference to any specific claim that Koyré makes in these writings, which are not even listed for the interested reader.

It is Lakatos who spells out the importance of Koyré and of the notion of epistemic breaks for the Kuhnian model of scientific change: 'his [Kuhn's] intellectual debt is to Koyré rather than to Popper. Koyré showed that positivism gives bad guidance to the historian of science, for the history of physics can only be understood in the context of a succession of "metaphysical" research programmes. Thus scientific changes are connected with vast cataclysmic metaphysical revolutions. Kuhn develops this message of Burtt and Koyré and the vast success of his book was partly due to his hard-hitting, direct criticism of justificationist historiography – which created a sensation among ordinary scientists and historians of science whom Burtt's, Koyré's (or Popper's) message has not yet reached' (Imre Lakatos, 'Falsification and the Methodology of Scientific Research Programmes', In Imre Lakatos and Alan Musgrave (eds), *Criticism and the Growth of Knowledge*, (Cambridge: Cambridge University Press, 1970) p. 92, n. 3.

A friend has suggested to me an interesting connection between Chomsky's *Syntactic Structures* (The Hague: Mouton, 1957) and Kuhn's *Structure of Scientific Revolutions*. Both Chomsky and Kuhn were Junior Fellows at Harvard in the fifties, Kuhn just prior to Chomsky. Chomsky's semantically meaningful counterpart of his famous example of a syntactically acceptable but nonsensical sentence, 'Colorless green ideas sleep furiously', was an entirely Kuhnian proposition, 'Revolutionary new ideas appear infrequently'.

28. It is thus perhaps via a Hopkins connection that Koyré's notion of radical breaks in thought has through Kuhn reappeared in a vulgar and popularised form in literary studies as the theory of competing institutionally determined ideologies. See, for instance, Stanley Fish's *Is There a Text in this Class?* (Cambridge, Mass.: Harvard University Press, 1980).

Kuhn's own version of the revolutionary model is toned down or flattened by having the divisions between paradigms filled in by what Kuhn calls 'normal science'. See the debate between Kuhn, Popper, and others, on the subject of normal science in *Criticism and the Growth of Knowledge*.

29. See Milner, 'Lacan and the Ideal of Science', forthcoming p. 2. It should be made clear that writing is quite distinct as a notion from language.

30. Milner, 'Lacan and the Ideal of Science' p. 6.

31. Milner, 'Lacan and the Ideal of Science', p. 7.

32. For a discussion of the real, see the entry under 'IMAGINARY, SYMBOLIC, REAL' in the glossary provided in the 'Translator's Note' to the Sheridan translation of the *Ecrits*, p. x.

33. Jacques Lacan, *The Four Fundamental Concepts of Psycho-Analysis*, Alan Sheridan (trans.) (New York: W. W. Norton, 1978) p. 4.

34. See Session 5, 'Tuchè and Automaton'. Lacan comments on it as follows: 'First, the *tuchè*, which we have borrowed, as I told you last time, from Aristotle, who uses it in his search for cause. We have translated it as *the encounter with the real*. The real is beyond the

automaton, the coming-back, the insistence of the signs, by which we see ourselves governed by the pleasure principle. The real is that which always lies beyond the automaton, and it is quite obvious, throughout Freud's research, that it is this that is the object of his concern' (pp. 53–4).

35. It is thus that I render the French *rencontre* in order to stress the randomness of the meeting.

36. One can also see Popper's notion of falsifiability as formulated to avoid the same problem.

37. Each time a rule predicting a wide range of data in the form of acceptable and non-acceptable strings by generating the former and excluding the latter requires the category 'noun phrase', for instance, to achieve the most elegant statement of the regularity it means to represent, the category receives yet another justification. See Saussure, *Course*, p. 38.

38. *Four Fundamental Concepts*, p. 55.

39. Milner, 'Lacan and the Ideal of Science', p. 7. Popper thus represents the meeting of rationalism and logical empiricism.

40. It is in this way that I take Lakatos's claim that theories may contain falsified propositions, for it is theories that must be falsifiable, not empirical claims.

41. Jean Hyppolite, 'L'Epistémologie de G. Bachelard', *Revue d'Histoire des Sciences* (Paris: PUF, Tome XVII, no. 1, January 1964) p. 5.

42. See G. Frege, 'Sense and Reference', in Peter Geach and Max Black (trans.), *Translations from the Philosophical Writings of Gottlob Frege*, (Oxford: Oxford University Press) p. 60, and Banfield, 'Describing the Unobserved: Events Grouped around an Empty Centre', in *The Linguistics of Writing* (Manchester: Manchester University Press, 1987) pp. 264–85.

43. D. F. Pears and B. F. McGuinness (trans), *Tractatus Logico–Philosophicus*, (London and Henley: Routledge & Kegan Paul, 1961) p. 5.

44. See, on the subject, Ian Hacking's *The Emergence of Probability* (Cambridge: Cambridge University Press, 1975).

45. As an example, take the way certain issues peculiar to syntactic theory are defined in a recent book by Joseph Emonds:

'In contrast, the grammatical formative category that characteristically appears with N, namely DET (determiner), is a *daughter*, not a sister to NP, and similarly for the grammatical category of DEG (degree words) that appears with A. Within the bar notation, this asymmetry follows from my proposal that V, but not N, A, or P, has a third projection in the bar notation. For in the bar notation, each lexical category X is paired with a corresponding grammatical formative category SP(X), called a specifier, which is a daughter to the maximal projection of X. If $S = V^3$, then we can take INFLECTION to be the specifier of V, and it follows that it is the sister to VP ($=V^2$), while SP(N) and SP(A) are daughters to NP and AP'. *A Unified Theory of Syntactic Categories* (Dordrecht:Foris Publications, 1985) p. 5. The specificity of these claims to a science whose object is language is in no way incompatible with traditional grammar, from which the notion of the grammatical categories in question is inherited. Nor should the formal language of the selection be confused by the reader unfamiliar with the real content of linguistics with jargon.

For a version of the analogising which does not observe the autonomy of each science, see Milner's account of Jakobson on Japanese metrics cited in this Introduction (pp. 36).

46. Roland Barthes, *Camera Lucida* (New York: Hill & Wang, 1981) p. 71.
47. Marcel Proust, *The Past Recaptured*, Andreas Mayor (trans.) (New York: Random House, 1971) p. 139. For the interested reader, the word here translated as 'magical scrawl' appears in Proust's original as the French word *grimoire* (see *A la Recherche du Temps Perdu III*, Paris: Gallimard, 1954, p. 879), a word which appears as well on several occasions in Milner's text. There is no single English word which implies, as *grimoire* does, something at once written and the repository of an abstruse knowledge. In translating it, I use on one occasion a line from Poe, on the author's suggestion. The word *grimoire* is etymologically related to the word *grammar*.
48. In generative grammar, the distinction between the acceptable and the non-acceptable divides the evidence provided by speakers' judgements; the division between the grammatical and the non-grammatical holds at the level of grammatical theory. 'Acceptability is a concept that belongs to the study of performance, whereas grammaticalness belongs to the study of competence'. Noam Chomsky, *Aspects of the Theory of Syntax* (Cambridge, Mass.: MIT Press, 1965) p. 11. The rules predict those sentences which are grammatical and exclude those which are not; by and large, those sentences generated by the grammar correspond with those judged acceptable, but there are exceptions. See Carlos-Peregrin Otero, 'Acceptable Ungrammatical [utterances] in Spanish',*Linguistic Inquiry*, 3 (1972) pp. 233–42, and 'Agrammaticality in Performance', *Linguistic Inquiry*, 4 (1973) pp. 551–62.
49. Michel Foucault, *The Order of Things* (New York: Random House, 1970) p. 235.
50. 'Milner's Reply', in *GLOW Newsletter*, 1 (September 1978) pp. 5–8.
51. Accepting this position of Freud's is not incompatible with holding that in some cases of hysteria a real seduction may have taken place or even that the real desire in question might be that of someone other than the hysteric – the writer of the case history, for instance. But it should be clear that in Freud's theory, *desire* is not imagined, but only something else that masks this desire.
52. On the subject of the disappearance of grammar in the intellectual tradition in English, see my '*Ecriture*, Narration and the Grammar of French', in Jeremy Hawthorn (ed.), *Narrative: From Malory to Motion Pictures, Stratford-upon-Avon Studies* (London: Edward Arnold, 1985) especially pp. 17–8.
53. Cf. Descartes's statement in the *Discourse on the method*: 'But even the best minds have no reason to desire to be acquainted with these principles, for if they wish to be able to talk of everything and acquire

a reputation for learning, they will more readily attain their end by contenting themselves with the appearance of truth which may be found in all sorts of things without much trouble, than in seeking for truth which only reveals itself little by little in certain spheres, and which, when others come into question, obliges one to confess one's ignorance. If, however, they prefer the knowledge of some small amount of truth to the vanity of seeming ignorant of nothing, which knowledge is doubtless preferable, or if they desire to follow a course similar to my own, it is not necessary that I should say any more than what I have already said in this Discourse'. *The Philosophical Works of Descartes*, vol. I, Elizabeth Haldane and G. R. T. Ross (trans.) (Cambridge: Cambridge University Press, 1967) pp. 125–6.

54. See my 'Linguistic Competence and Literary Theory', in John Fisher (ed.),*Essays in Aesthetics* (Philadelphia: Temple University Press, 1983) pp. 201–34.

55. For the interested reader, there is only one place in the text where I have not capitalised the translation of *langage*, and that is in the word *metalanguage*. The language of the title and of Chapter 7 is with a small *l*.

56. *The Order of Things*, pp. 236 and 235.

57. See *The Order of Things*, Chapters 7 and 8.

58. According to Foucault, this change is first apparent in the attention focused on inflections by comparative, historical grammar: 'Now a new element intervenes: on the one hand, on the side of meaning or representation, it indicates only an accessory and necessarily secondary value . . . ; on the other hand, on the side of form, it constitutes the solid, constant, almost inalterable totality whose sovereign law is so far imposed upon the representative [i.e., representational] roots as to modify even those roots themselves. Moreover, this element, secondary in its significative value, primary in its formal consistence, is not itself an isolated syllable, like a sort of constant root; it is a system of modifications of which the various segments are interdependent: . . .

'Until the end of the eighteenth century, this new analysis has its place in the search for the representative [representational] values of language. It is still a question of discourse. But already, through the inflectional system, the dimension of the purely grammatical is appearing: language no longer consists only of representations and of sounds that in turn represent the representations and are ordered among them as the links of thought require; it consists also of formal elements, grouped into a system, which impose upon the sounds, syllables, and roots an organization that is not that of representation'. *The Order of Things*, p. 235.

59. In Chomsky, one version of arbitrariness is the autonomy of syntax, presented in *Syntactic Structures*. This is what Dan Sperber and Deirdre Wilson call the '*sui generis*' nature of linguistic structure, with a reference to *Syntactic Structures*. See Dan Sperber and Deirdre Wilson, *Relevance: Communication and Cognition* (Cambridge, Mass.: Harvard University Press, 1986) p. 8.

60. 'It is first in this sense that Lacan created this word, added it to the language, *"lalangue"*, in a single word thus uniting the definite article, the singular to the very name or vocable. We will say like him "les lalangue", "chaque [every] lalangue,", because no *lalangue* is comparable to any other'. J.-A. Miller, 'Théorie de Lalangue', *Ornicar*, 1 (January 1975) p. 26.
61. *Encore*, p. 132.
62. Milner, 'Renaissance et Jakobson', *Cahiers de Poétique Comparée X*, 1985, pp. 61–6.

Preface

The Freudian field is coextensive with the field of speech. But speech itself does not extend in all directions, ceaselessly coming up as it does against the fact that not everything can be said.

For there is an impossible peculiar to language, one which returns always to its place, which some – those called 'purists' – will go so far as to fall in love with: the 'do's and don't's', the rule, Vaugelas's sovereignty of usage, otherwise called a *real*. This real speaking beings have to come to terms with – so what is so surprising if they try their hand in the true sense at domesticating it, by this art of love which is called grammar, by this science which is called linguistics?

Between the art and the science, the limit is marked by an axiom which the first denies and by means of which the second maintains itself. The real of language is of the order of the calculable. But one cannot arrive directly at the axiom itself; what is required is:

(1) That language be constituted as a real, be made its own cause, in setting aside every cause which is not of its order, in making it a cause only of its own order. This is what is called the arbitrariness of the sign, by which is only meant that the sign cannot have any master other than itself, and is master only of itself.

(2) That language be constituted as a real representable for calculation, as a real for which the small letters of a formalisation may be substituted. This is what the concept of the sign and the principle of distinctiveness is for: each segment, each unit of language – word, sentence, sound, meaning – understood as a sign, is represented in a manner univocal and analysable, identity for identity, difference for difference.

51

(3) That of the speaking being there be retained in general only what makes it the support of something calculable, that it be thought of as a point without division or extension, with neither past nor future, neither a consciousness nor an unconscious, without a body – and without any other desire except to articulate. This is the angel who has from time immemorial been the image of what becomes of a subject when nothing of it is retained but the dimension of pure enunciation.

(4) That of the multiplicity of speaking beings there be retained only what is necessary to constitute a real calculable as a language: two points, let us say, one of emission, the other of reception, two symmetrical points, endowed with the same properties, hence indistinguishable, except by their numerical duality. This is what the concept of communication accomplishes.

Thus is constructed the system of the real from calculation to calculation with, as its only principle of investigation, the impossible, understood as the agrammatical. What is surprising is its success.

Psychoanalysis plays in this only one role of importance: to state that when it comes to language, science may fail. To which science can scarcely object, for things do not work in linguistics as in logic. The real which underlies it is not sutured; it is crisscrossed with faults – and they are perceptible by science itself.

These lines of fault cross and overlap. Calculation identifies them as what is irreducible to calculation, but it is not another system that they delineate, on which one could construct a new, unheard-of science – the vanity of grammatologies. Yet their nature and their logic can be illuminated by Freudian discourse; in *lalangue*, conceived henceforth as unrepresentable by calculation – that is to say as crystal – they are the recesses where desire flashes and the thrill comes to settle.

Thus I announced in 1974 a series of lectures that I planned to give in the department of psychoanalysis at Vincennes. I was then in the process of drafting, for academic purposes, a strictly syntactic work – surprised, no doubt, to find myself brought to this extremity, but surprised also not to be more bored. So, the suspicion sometimes came to me: could it be possible that linguistics interested me?

As far as grammar was concerned, I knew the answer, since I had constantly been able time and again to observe how, tired of work which required originality and invention, I revived myself by tasks having to do purely with language: translations or philological commentaries. But nothing followed from this so far as linguistics was concerned, which I have long held to be only a substitute, imposed by a hard modernity, for this grammar now fallen into discredit. And, here I had caught myself becoming attached to the science which accredited me in the world. This went against all expectations and merited questioning myself about.

No doubt I could have maintained that, in this move, I was motivated only by an epistemological concern; if, after all, linguistics is a science, is it not precisely when a practitioner gives himself over to it in detail, that he should return to the foundations and apply himself to expounding them in the conceptual language which best suits his purposes? But this would have been, I saw well enough, to distort the facts. On the one hand, because I scarcely believed in epistemology – if Koyré and Lacan are right, if science since Galileo is only a domain characterised for observation by the combination of two features: the constitution of a 'mathematicisable' writing and the validation of every successful technique – then the fundamental epistemological question, 'is such a given set of propositions *a* science?', is revealed as no less than frivolous; it suffices to establish if these propositions belong to the domain of *science* – that is to say, present the requisite characteristics. No doubt, certain epistemologists have tried in the recent past to take comfort in a political imperative – for if it is necessary for Marxism to belong to science, it becomes clear that science can no longer be defined along modern lines. Where is Marxism's writing, where is the technique it would validate? In that case, one would have to have recourse to the classic criteria, scarcely modified from Aristotle: a good definition of the domain, of the object, of the concepts, of the axioms, in short the normal paraphernalia. But for some time now political imperatives no longer carry the same weight. If in fact Marxism did have some truth, did it have for that reason to belong to science? Was there not some prejudice here, in fact the modern prejudice *par excellence* – that the locus of all validity can only be science? As far as knowing whether Marxism has arrived at any truth, we will let this question pass. Nothing any longer prevented all epistemological questions from being reduced to their simple form; but, in the case of linguistics, it is particularly easy today – let us say, after Chomsky – to establish its inclusion in the domain of Galilean writing – which, moreover, has no great consequences, unless to establish the exact relation that it maintains with grammar.

Even if I still attributed some importance to epistemology, it was not in any case what occupied me at this juncture. I was in fact called upon by circumstances to turn to the very area of language where something presenting itself as a scientifically expressible rule interested me. On this issue also, I had once had a ready answer. Convinced that the intellectual animals, as in Kipling's jungle, let themselves be guided by a master-word which it sufficed only to utter and by means of which every imaginable proposition is ultimately measured, I had imagined that at various historical periods this word proceeded from different points: from theology, of course, but its hour had passed; philosophy, on the other hand, was then – circa 1960 – in full flowering, but my small inclination for original ideas kept me from a discipline where they dominate. There remained grammar. It is after all true that grammar has from a certain point of view universal jurisdiction over every proposition: all that was necessary then was to keep to this point of view in order to raise the standards of an absolute monarchy over the various discourses. Discovering once more the structure of a medieval dispute, but resolving it by default, I had looked to grammar for what philosophy seemed to deny me. It is no doubt true that I have subsequently found other resources in epistemology, which by definition summons every proposition and measures it by the master-word of science and of theory, or in politics, whose peculiarity in France is to accord itself universal power of validation and invalidation. Even so, however, grammar, even under its modern form as science, had remained as a minor but certain possibility, more especially as it was widely held that linguistics had carried out the destiny of all the sciences of man.

But, in 1974, I no longer believed any of this. Not only had philosophy, not only had politics dissolved in smoke in the direction of some lunar region, but the real had radically disappeared. There is no master-word – because there is a Master; because there is an infinity of words, all and none, at the whim of fortune, able to serve the discourse of this master; because, finally, there is no universality of discourses. And yet, linguistics held out, and what is more, resisted on its own and no longer as grammar's recent avatar. From whence came, once again, this resistance and this unexpected dividend of a desire?

Only one approach was open: to try to establish if there is some sense in speaking of a desire of the linguist as such, then to try to name it – that is to say, to articulate the ways by which a speaking being can be enrolled in support of a science having for its ground what makes for the existence of a speaking being, and for its object some area of this ground. A form of wild self-analysis, perhaps, but guaranteed nevertheless by the signifiers of a Lacanian approach, which forbids everything and anything from being uttered. I appropriated these signifiers in order to interrogate the science in which I discovered that I was indeed inscribed as subject – perhaps this is what some would call Lacanian epistemology; incorrectly, however, since at this juncture what matters is only the knotting together of a desire and of certain phrases which happen also to qualify as belonging to science.

The lectures which I was announcing were given in the course of the first half of 1974–5 and, as was to be expected, were not without their effect on the one who delivered them – so much so that (rereading one day the announcement that I had drawn up for them) it became clear to me that a greater precision was possible, and desirable. It did not seem advisable not somehow to indicate this. In any case, not giving in to the demands of anyone, except myself, I wrote out my lectures and asked the journal *Ornicar*, which consented, to publish them – semi-publication, in fact, whose guardedness answered to the tentative quality of my resolve. Moreover, the testimony of certain individuals, translators or poets known themselves to be interested in language, no less than the embarrassed silence of a few scatterbrains, all assured me that I had, however obscurely, hit upon some truth. Hence arose the desire to publish elsewhere, accentuated perhaps by a disingenuous need to make it easier for me to take.

But, as we know, one does not pass unhindered from what was clandestine to a more open form. I neither wished nor was able to take up again without modification the *Ornicar* text. On the other hand, this text did not cease to exist, and there was a shade of deceit attached to stretching it out by here and there inserting afterthoughts. Furthermore, certain observations of Deleuze and Guattari, in their *Rhizome*[1], had their effect on me – did we need, in fact, branching or linear books? I preferred thus to rely upon the approximate and the heterogeneous, to retain the *Ornicar* text with the exception of certain minor revisions but to insert in it at three points a detour, recalling, anticipating, shifting what comes from that text – at times correcting it, at times confirming it in other ways. In short, a little flurry of activity, but not too much, because one does have one's taboos.

Note

1.   Paris: Minuit, 1976.

1

Fore-Word

We are presented with a set of realities that we call *languages*. In fact, we scarcely hesitate to attribute this name to them, each and all, as if we always had at our disposal a rule allowing us, once a reality is given, to determine whether or not it belongs to the particular set. This assumes inevitably certain defining properties, common to all the elements which merit the name of 'language' and exclusively represented by these latter. If by abstraction an autonomous being is conferred on these properties, what is called 'Language' is obtained, nothing more in itself than a point starting from which the various languages can be grouped together into a whole, but a point on which extension is conferred in ascribing expressible properties to it.

But this moment of Language only thematises an anterior operation, for to speak of 'languages' is perhaps already at the very least to conceive of them as capable of being grouped together; in the drift which relates languages to Language, a proposition must henceforth be reinstated: 'languages form a consistent class,' a class such then that its elements can be thought of *all together* without contradiction.[1]

This is then what our words tell us, but we take from them the opposite as well – who cannot see that the class of languages can be said to be inconsistent, since there is always one of its elements such that it cannot be proposed without being revealed as incommensurate with all the others? This language that it is customary to call 'maternal' can always be taken in a way that prevents it from being counted along with other languages, from being added to them, compared to them. But once that has been established, what prevents our taking all languages in this light and considering them as radically incapable of being totalised, that which makes them alike becoming that which renders them incommensurate?

But we say much more in saying 'languages'. Certainly we assume them to be several and grouped together, but also that it is always possible to distinguish between them. For this plural is actually a collection of singulars, at one and the same time alike and discernible. In other words, we hold that there is always a sense in speaking of *a* language, so that one can always, for any segment whatever, decide if it belongs to this language or not. Yet nothing is less sure. Granting even that we can always know for a given segment of reality how to decide if it is part of language or not, it does not follow that one can always assign it to one language rather than to another. Alongside the usual cases where the distinction is trivial, there are ones where identity and differences become confused – what of the case where there are different types of syntax from which a single subject can occasionally choose according to his or her humour or circumstances? Or that of two subjects, convinced they are speaking the same language, whose judgements of grammaticality can nevertheless be observed to diverge constantly? Or the case of dialects, of 'levels of language'?

That it may not be possible to decide whether two languages are identical or not would still be unimportant if one could always be assured that every construction – and thereby every language as a set of constructions – were identical to itself. No doubt there are elementary precautions which permit us to skirt the immediate difficulties – thus it is necessary at least to avoid letting the merest accidental occurrence obscure the flash of the identical. Let us agree then to call 'language' this kernel which, in each one of the various languages supports its uniqueness and its distinctness; it cannot be represented on the side of substance, indefinitely overburdened with diverse accidents, but only as a form, invariable across its actualisations, since it is defined in terms of relations.[2] We recognise here the schism between language and speech, *langue* and *parole*, which device, whether openly or not, functions in all the usual versions of linguistics. The operation is thus possible; yet nonetheless it does not fail to arouse suspicion when it is observed that it is always also possible – without departing from immediate experience – to bring into focus in every grammatical construction a non-identical dimension. This is the equivocal and all that arises from it – homophony, homosemy, homography – all that supports the *double entendre* and the innuendo, continuous fabric of our conversations.

For it is easy to see that a grammatical construction, embroidered by equivocation, is at the same time itself and another. Its uniqueness is refracted in the direction of those series which elude the operation of deduction, since each one, no sooner named – meaning, sonority, writing, etymology, syntax, pun . . . – is refracted in turn indefinitely – not the tree which calculates this multiplicity, but the crystal of the aleph, by means of which Borges perhaps intends to metaphorise the non-identical location, where every speaking being, as such, takes its place. And one can in turn understand in Saussure's celebrated assertion 'language is a form and not a substance' the formula which saves the identical, the substance of language revealing finally what it is: what is non-identical to itself.

No doubt, one can expel the equivocal by well-defined procedures. If it is out of the sound that it is constituted, by resorting to the sense; if it is out of the sense, by resorting to the sound; if it is out of writing, etc., in a word, by relying on the fact that *there are stratas*. We will grant, then, that the phonemes articulate the words and distinguish them, that the words articulate the phrases; and the phrases, the sentences. By this operation, types and orders are introduced, in a way so similar to the Russellian method that one would think the latter was a simple repetition of what grammars have always known. And just as paradoxes consist only in the confusion of types, so also the equivocal dissolves in a phantom born of the unwarranted conjunction of several strata: it explodes in combined univocables. But suppose in exchange that one confines oneself to experience: in the grammatical construction, whether it is spoken or written or heard or read, it is by abstraction that the stratas are distinguished. This difference which makes 'Paris' at one and the same time a noun phrase, a noun, a sequence of phonemes, makes it able to be understood as mention or as use, is one that is in no way required, if not by the demand that language not be equivocal – imaginary circle where what makes possible the satisfaction of the demand has no other foundation than the demand itself.

But the real of the equivocal resists; language does not cease to be destratified by it. More especially as, in comparison with language itself, there is no lack of points where stratification is suspended. Their inventory, for being incomplete, is not unknown. Personal pronouns, performatives, insults, exclamations – all elements whose definition in mention involves circularly the use of the *definiendum*, whose meaning cannot be entirely explained without recourse to the very uttering of it: 'I', as we know, designates the one who says 'I,' 'to swear' is to say 'I swear', etc. Certainly that does not affect the possibility of a regular account. In order for language to be constructed, it suffices for these elements outside the orbit of the ordinary to be relegated to its farthest limit by an adequate naming. But even this is not accomplished without loss. It will be necessary from now on to admit into the ether of language heterogenous singularities.

Now language is clearly conceived only in absolute isotopy: from whatever point it is considered, it must present the same physiognomy. But this is what is not confirmed by the simplest data; in the series of homogeneous places, some singularities are revealed.

A language, as the possible object of a proposition which can be universally validated – and, even more importantly, of any writing that is scientific – claims to be always distinguishable from what is not a language, always distinguishable from another language, always identical to itself, always inscribable in the sphere of univocableness, and always an isotope. In short, it must be *One*. But the result is that these irreducible conditions are satisfied only by setting aside certain propositions:

- languages do not form a consistent class, being incommensurable;
- a language is not identical to itself;
- a language is a substance;
- a language can cease to be stratified;
- a language is not an isotope.

But, as we have seen, nothing in experience renders any of these propositions impossible to maintain; it is by a principled decision that they are set aside and this principle is reduced to the simple demand that a certain type of universalisable proposition be stated for every language.

This is not all, for these five propositions which have been set aside do not fail to delineate, if they are taken as a whole, a certain site of language, some real which insists in each one and that linguistics or grammar have agreed to deny. This insistent element indeed belongs to the order of languages; what is more, it does not entirely escape the senses since it is out of experience itself that the encounter with it can be described, so much so that to set it aside is simply to proceed by abstraction. It remains then to name this ferret which passes through the five propositions and whose projected shadow only we have thus far seized. But here the difficulty takes on a further complication. Should it be so surprising that no name for it readily presents itself, since every name aims at univocableness? No univocal designation then for the site of equivocations. Only a semblance can be provided for it – one itself highly wrought by the equivocal for which the real is here made the target. It can be seen why *lalangue*, the name forged by Lacan, is appropriate.[3]

Lalangue is thus one language among others, to the extent that once postulated, it prevents by incommensurability the construction of a class of languages which includes it; its most direct figuration is indeed the mother tongue, for which little observation suffices to recognise that in every hypothesis a marked distortion is required to include it in the common lot. But it is at the same time any language, insofar as all are, under some aspect, one among others and, for some speaking being, a mother tongue. Not that the distinctive character on which the incommensurability of a language is based can be stated in linguistic propositions; on the contrary, the incommensurability vanishes the moment one adopts the point of view which would permit such propositions. In other words, *lalangue* is what makes one language not comparable to any other, insofar as it has precisely no other, insofar also as what makes it incomparable could not be said.

Lalangue is, in every language, the register which consigns it to the equivocal. We know how to arrive at it: by destratifying, by confusing systematically sound and sense, mention and use, writing and the represented, in preventing thereby one strata from serving as a means for extricating another. But one must be careful here – this register is none other than what distinguishes one language absolutely from every other, the particularity of any given language resulting only from the series where its uniqueness is undone. What one language is among others, then, is nothing more than a singular way of producing equivocation. It becomes thereby a collection of sites, all singular and all heterogeneous: from whatever perspective one considers it, it is other to itself, constantly heterotopic. In this way, it becomes substance as well, the possible material for phantasies, the inconsistent set of sites for desire. Language is then what in practice the unconscious is, lending itself to all imaginable games, so that truth, under the sway of words, speaks.

Lalangue is all this; access to it is thus via a negative route starting from everyday words – 'language' (*langue*), 'Language' (*langage*) – and the use that we make of them is readily translatable into theory. Once postulated, it appears, nevertheless, as that of which these everyday words are the purification and the adulteration. One can then proceed via the positive route and situate Language with a capital *L* and language with a small *l*, starting out from *lalangue*. To *lalangue* Language lends the features which lead the former back toward consistency and class membership; at the same time, Language inserts *lalangue* in the whole or all of realities where it finds its place and distinctiveness. Likewise, the speaking being is conceived as a whole or all, distinguished by the fact that it speaks – this human race, whose essential attribute is Language. It is easy enough, for anyone who wishes to do so, to mark here the imaginary drift: does Language depend in effect on anything other than on this moment when the speaking being apprehends itself reflexively as having others like it, fellow beings, who together form a class with it and are distinguished within a universe? In short, has it any other basis than the mirror and the image of its *like*ness there constructed? (see Chapter 8, footnote 2).

As for language, it is not itself without the effect of drift; preserving identity with itself, does it not confer on *lalangue* what it requires for any collection whatever of speaking beings to continue to exist? Namely, the minimum of permanence that every contract requires and for which writing readily supplies the support. Is this to say that language must be credited entirely to the account of the imaginary? That is what many would claim; but need one go so far as to concede that grammars and dictionaries, that writing as such all testify to nothing more than the empty-display to which in actual fact they often lend themselves? In other words again, is not language a mask arbitrarily constructed, one which touches upon no real? Such is indeed the uncertainty which gnaws at linguists, once the real effectiveness of psychoanalysis ceases to be unknown to them; it is of little importance to them if Language (*langage*) is nothing but drift, for only language (*langue*) counts in their eyes. And this to the point that in language everything is at stake for them. For if it were absolutely true that language touched upon no real, it would be the linguist's desire which would find itself reduced to a hollow mockery. Conversely, if the opinions circulating about language are not well founded, they all work toward one purpose only – to make linguists abandon their desire.

The project of clarifying the relation between *lalangue* and language hence touches on ethics.

Notes

1. Cf. J. A. Miller, 'Théorie de lalangue', *Ornicar*, 1 (January, 1975) pp. 27–8. The source is Cantor's letter to Dedekind, dated July 1899, in Cantor, *Abhandlungen Mathematischen u. Philosophischen Inhalts* (Olms Verlag: Hildeshein, 1966) pp. 443–4.
2. Whether these relations be those that Saussure – and structuralism after him – has described as paradigmatic and syntagmatic, or whether they be written as rules of a diverse nature is of little importance.
3. I refer in particular to 'L'Etourdit' (*Scilicet* 4, Paris: Seuil, 1973) and to the last session of *Encore* – as well as to the commentary of J. A. Miller, 'Théorie de lalangue', pp. 16–34.

2

The Production of Language with a Small *l*

Linguistics, insofar as it is affected by the possibility of psycho-analysis, will be our object. Hence the title that we have chosen: the key to it is simple and consists in the conjunction of common terms that have simply been taken literally. What must language actually be that one can designate it equally as the object of a science and the object of a love?

We offer in response three hypotheses:

- when one speaks of loving language, it is indeed a kind of love which is implied;
- the language of which it is a question is precisely that which linguistics must come to know;
- it is through this intersection that the point where desire comes to corrupt a human science can be discovered, where, if one is willing to take the necessary trouble, an intelligible relation is tied to a possible theory of desire.

The question then is: what is language if psychoanalysis exists?

But in saying *language* (*langue*), we evoke once more the series *langue*, *parole*, *langage*, that the French language proposes to us and that tradition imposes on us. We will avoid the effects of indeterminacy, too observable in the literature, only by determining a point for this set from which it can be 'constructed'. The series, in fact, like every other, takes its logic from the term which exceeds it and which it is meant to efface. This term, named by subterfuge, is *lalangue*, in other words, that by which, with one and the same stroke, there is language (or beings who can be qualified as speaking, which comes down to the same thing) and there is an unconscious.

Lalangue then will be taken as given. Language with a capital *L* designates what learning elaborates on the subject of *lalangue* – and notably on that of its existence, so that the concept of Language consists quite entirely in the question: 'Why is there *lalangue* rather than nothing?' In other words, Language is nothing other than *lalangue* taken at the juncture of its existence or non-existence – a learning that passes through the phantasmic absence of its object. This is moreover why Language is always concerned with hypotheses about origins, this last being the moving image of the immoving juncture, the narrative form where absence and presence are successively articulated.

Language with a small *l* is something else. Unlike Language, it does not turn on existence as such, but on the modality of existence; the question that this term sums up is 'why is language like it is and not otherwise?', which quite evidently presupposes another: 'What is language like?', and an answer contained in a 'it is like this', which simply ignores the question of what could be the foundation of its existence and imagines nothing of a possible inexistence. This is why, moreover, reciprocally, those who are concerned with language with a small *l* set aside all investigation of its origin. For understanding the 'it is like this', one apparently simple way is open: *lalangue* once more. The fact of language consists in there being in *lalangue* the impossible – the impossible to say, the impossible not to say in a certain way. One readily recognises here the partitioning separating the correct and the incorrect which is at the heart of grammars and linguistic descriptions.[1] From that point on, language in itself is nothing other than this partitioning considered from a general point of view, *a* language is a particular form of it, a dialect of a language, a specific reorganisation of a particular partitioning.

But this simplicity is deceptive, for the true nature of the partitioning is covered over with the litter of imaginary substitutes: the most familiar and the most dangerous consists in utilising the Language of mastery, to understand the impossible as an obligation, dependent on a sovereign – whether a contract, a caprice, a tacit consensus. It is known moreover that from time immemorial dictators, from Caesar to Stalin, have preoccupied themselves with language, recognising in it the most faithful image of a naked power, which does not even have to name itself. Conversely, the cause of liberty seems to concern itself with denouncing the artifice of grammars and the vanity of their rules, to the point of maintaining that language knows no impossible.[2]

Let us leave for an instant the obvious case of the Language of mastery and confine ourselves to the minimum – to speak of language and of partitioning is to postulate that everything, that all, cannot be said. In other words, the pure concept of language is that of a not-all marking *lalangue* – or, to put it otherwise, language is what sustains *lalangue* insofar as it is not-all.

Let us reconsider what Lacan, in *Télévision*, has made to function as the starting point of his discourse: the truth is not all said, and that because the words for it are wanting, words fail. The proposition that he extracts from this, by equivalence, is that the truth, insofar as it is not-all, touches upon the real.

But this reading cannot stop here. From the fact that the truth may not all be said, one can also conclude that the truth is nothing other than that for which words are wanting. Now, words are always wanting, and the not-all which marks the truth insofar as it should be said, marks also *lalangue*, insofar as every true statement passes by way of it. From whence it follows that, like the truth itself, *lalangue* touches upon the real.

Hence, the thesis that language sustains *lalangue* insofar as it is not-all is directly translated by: *language sustains the real of lalangue*.

On the question of whether language is linked to the operation of the not-all, it is not difficult, despite appearances, to recover the traces handed down through tradition. After all, the myth of Babel says nothing else – since it links the possibility of language to that of a division indefinite and incapable of being added up.[3] In the same way, Saussure constructs the myth of two continuums (two streams) which are conjoined and which, by this very meeting, find themselves divided, each being found to exceed the other and to doom it to be found wanting. We know finally that tradition has handed down to grammarians the list of the parts of speech. It is not difficult to demonstrate their fictional status, but the overly critical do not realise that in this case what is important is not so much the exact list of the parts as the fact that some parts of speech are always and necessarily presupposed. One can argue over whether the line must be drawn between noun and verb, but that the line must be drawn somewhere there can be no doubt. In other words, as we already find in Plato (*Sophist*, 262a), language, even if one imagines it as a numberable totality, is also necessarily marked by the heterogeneous and the non-superimposable.

By contrast, one can go on failing to recognise that language belongs to the order of the real – for example, by translating language in terms of reality, situating it in the system of the useful as an instrument of communication or in the system of 'practices' – social or otherwise. Or, to take another example, the real of language is measured by the clinical chart of neuroses to describe the dialects of the hysteric, of the obsessional, and so on, having at the same time passed off for the real the phantasies pieced together from its fragments.

Nonetheless, the issues at stake in the diverse discourses on language do indeed impinge on the status of this real. The main partitioning can be summed up as follows: *the real is conceived as representable or not.*

This partitioning contains nothing that is actually specific; it articulates in its most general form the very meeting of the real with the speaking being. Suppose, in fact, that the real exists – something, moreover, that no *logic* could predict. All that subjects, if they encounter it, *ask* of it, is for somehow a representation to be possible. Only at this price with which the imaginary ransoms it will subjects be able to support what, in itself, escapes them. But, two conditions must be added: that for subjects the repeatable must exist, and this repeatable must form a system. Upon the first all writing is founded; by the second, all writing acquires the property of being consistent that belongs to the representable.

There is no shortage of such representations, to be sure, but for modern man, the only ones which count are those which can qualify as belonging to the order of science. In other words, they must be formulated as *theories*, where the scraps of writing inscribing some bits and pieces of the real are sewn back together in a figure which receives its value on the basis of a certain whole or all and holds for all. The difficulty is that, in itself, modern science proposes no representation, imposes no theory; it limits itself to offering writings. What can guarantee that, over and above this, the theories of the universe, that the universe itself, understood as a system, will be more than phantasies? But, in the case of language, we can be more confident, reassured by a two-step procedure where grammar, laying out at one and the same time the repeatable and the systematic, guarantees in advance its scientific status. To maintain that the real of language is representable is in effect the initial step of every grammar. It consists in recognising the impossible peculiar to language in the existence of the repeatable,[4] and, furthermore, in constituting it as a system – this is what is called the *regular*. As a result the real can be the object of rules and tables which map out its features. Linguistics then adds only this: the representation enters the orbit of science.

The science in question is indeed modern science, that which, in the wake of Galileo, substitutes for the object letters or symbols in terms of which it develops its arguments. That this might be possible for any language at all has only recently been suspected. Actually, as Saussure realised by the time of his *Mémoire* of 1878, it is comparative grammar which is decisive here,[5] and not, as one might have thought, philosophical grammars. The latter, in fact, were able to claim the status of science, not only that of Aristotle, but also that of Descartes and of Newton (the Preface of Beauzée's *Grammaire générale et raisonnée* can be profitably consulted on this point), but they never fulfilled the minimum requirement: the construction of a writing. Consider, by contrast, the comparative grammar of Indo-European. What is important is not that it works out historical sequences – it should be noted in fact that it never dates its forms and limits itself to establishing relations of order – but that it can *set down* forms, by definition non-observable, having the function of a matrix for a set of observed forms. The Indo-European root, combined according to phonetic laws, sets forth in n signs (in principle, three) a multiplicity of possible lexemes and each of the signs which spell it out sym-bolise an open series of phonetic correspondences. In short, comparative grammar consists of a writing governed by a structur-ing real – that this real must also be considered as anterior is at this point secondary.

I might add that the notion of 'kinship' between languages assumes that they have properties unaffected by what they com-municate and designate, for finally who would believe that a word in Greek, Sanskrit, Latin, Germanic, Tocharian, and so on, should have, even if structurally identical, the same referential value? We can therefore see why the *Course*, which is, if properly assessed, only the setting forth of the conceptual conditions making com-parative grammar possible, sets aside reference, isolates the formal and opens the way for a symbolic notation.

Once this was accomplished, it became as it were natural to refer these notations to the universal science of possible symbolisms, otherwise known as logic. This is essentially what Chomsky has done, replacing the patchwork writing of structuralism by a formalism completely assimilable into systems theory.

But the real of language has the peculiar property that it is not recognised in a univocal fashion, and 'regularity' can be held to be either its mask or its sign. The alternation is an ancient one; it is the basis of the quarrel between anomalists and analogists which divided the ancient grammars.[6] For the analogists, the effect of language results precisely from the proportionality, or analogy, which makes the general rules possible, everything which is not integrated into them being considered an exception, in other words, a parasite, a phantom presence in language of what is not language (but rather for example, tradition, which is what the archaism is, or rhetorical intention, which is what the figure is). For the anomalists, on the other hand, the general rules are the artifice, a rationalisation of professional grammarians. Language is recognised, conversely, as comprised of non-repeatable obligations, entirely idiosyncratic, in a word, anomalous. What was seen negatively as an exception is now the positivity of the real. From this point on the real becomes essentially non-representable – neither tables, nor general rules, nor, obviously, any symbolic writing, but only the simple assertion of an impossible: 'say this, but don't say that'.

If the real is not representable, language, as such, is not, in Lacan's sense, mathematicisable in terms of representation. There could not be, by the methods of any theory, the transmission of a matheme touching this real. If there is transmission, it consists properly in an initiation, passing along routes diversely named – the fact of belonging to an ethnic or social class, the 'honesty' of Vaugelas – but one always escaping reason, which is the figure of the subject presupposed in the matheme. On the contrary, the partisans of the representable are by that very position condemned to making pronouncements on the basis of the transmittable, whence the intrinsic relation they maintain with the school. One can thus see why grammatical tradition, especially in France, is divided into two entirely distinct branches. One, expressed in the form of complete and well-ordered treatises called grammars or syntaxes, is intended for the classroom; the other, presented in brief newspaper columns or in aphoristic books, is initiatory. That the initiated might turn out to be nothing more than the ludicrous set of average people alters nothing of its structure. The opposition is already that between Port-Royal and Vaugelas or Bouhours. It persists to this day (although there are points of overlap, the most characteristic being Grevisse). If we agree to call the partisans of the representable grammarians, the partisans of the unrepresentable could well be those called *purists*.

One can easily fail to recognise what is at stake in purism – nothing less than the fact that, being considered an unrepresentable real, language can function as *agalma*, treasure, the object (*a*). 'Purity' becomes the cause of a desire, and the purist is the subject to whom it gives a sign in language. Thus, it is actually a real love that we have to deal with, the very love of language, obvious source of ridicule when it calls attention to itself. This is why the purist, like the miser, is material for comedy, extracting from the cycle of the useful a treasure which is never worth anything.

For, unlike Harpagon's, the casket of the purists has always been missing. Nothing for them guarantees that they will preserve the purity of language, cause of their desire, nothing if not perhaps a kingdom of the dead, a lifeless collection of quotations by means of which authors are summoned up to speak the pure. While nothing requires grammarians themselves to apply the grammar they decree, purists must be pure in the very least of their sentences. Initiated into 'a quaint and curious volume of forgotten lore', they are its representatives on earth and first disciples. Each time they speak, their downfall awaits them, but if they escape it, they have victoriously crossed the Acheron only to bring back, like a modern Orpheus, a flower that the light immediately fades, the pure itself.

Such is the first figure of the love of language. We will not encounter it again, for it is what linguistics and grammar spend their time freeing themselves from. It should be kept in mind, however, for perhaps it reveals a power of language which flows from its essence.

APPENDED NOTE

Unlike language (*langue*), Language (*langage*) sums up a question of the following form: 'why is there X rather than nothing?' This type of question is known to be by definition a philosophical one, since it bears on the difference between an existence and that which is its basis. Language with a capital *L* belongs then structurally to the sphere of philosophy, and (in French) one speaks correctly only of 'philosophy of *langage*' and not of 'philosophy of *langue*'. In the same way, moreover, language not being situated at that juncture at which an inexistence turns into an existence, it does not give rise to accounts of its origin; one only properly speaks of 'the origin of *langage*' and not of 'the origin of *langue*.'

In this way, a chart of oppositions can be readily constructed which allows us to interpret texts as either bearing on Language or language, and especially to assign them to one category or the other. Interpretation is sometimes less easy than one would be led to believe. Take for example Horace's celebrated text, *The Art of Poetry*, lines 70–2:

> Multa renascentur quae jam cecidere, cadentque
> Quae nunc sunt in honore vocabula, si volet usus
> Quem penes arbitrium est et jus et norma loquendi

'Many words will be reborn which today have fallen from use, and many will fall from use which are at present in use, when usage so wills, for with it resides the power of judgement, the law and the rule'.

I translate *usus*' by 'usage', as is generally done, since this text is always cited as one of the first where the doctrine of the sovereignty of usage over language is expressed. It should be noted in passing that the three terms designating authority are not distributed randomly – *arbitrium* would seem to designate an actual power, operating in the realm of facts, *jus* is the written law, *norma* the current rule, with no other title than custom. These are then the three possible forms of authority in the Latin tradition, which in their entirety exhaust the figures of the master. In this traditional reading, Horace's text expresses a proposition about *langue*, as opposed to *langage*, since it is in no way a question of origins and, in point of fact, it seems to be inscribed in the figure that we have called attention to – to imagine in terms of mastery the partitioning which organises language, the correct being here conceived as *honos*, 'an official post', and language as the set of forms *in honore*, that is to say, 'in office'.

But M. Grimal, in his study of *The Art of Poetry*,[7] adopts a different position; his arguments are the following: (1) *usus* in the sense given it here is extremely rare, if not without example; (2)

72 *For the Love of Language*

Horace employs it elsewhere in relation to linguistic facts and doesn't give it this meaning. In this passage (*Sat.* I, 3, v. 102), *usus* designates the need which is at the origin of techniques, but also of words. As a result, the position comes down to the fact that words arise and disappear at the whim of need, and the same principle which is at the origin of Language (*langage*) governs its continued existence. But in this case the term *usus* contains within itself an implict thesis about origins, and the whole of the text of the *The Art of Poetry* bears not on *langue*, as is ordinarily believed, but on *langage*.[8]

Notes

1. To be more precise, there is a real border that the division of the correct and the incorrect represents. This is the relation itself that, following Lacan, sustains the not-all of the sexual relation, the divisions into sexed halves in which the *I*'s (egos) are caught. For another interpretation and a discussion of the homology between the two forms of borderline, cf. Judith Milner, 'Langage et langue – ou: de quoi rient les locuteurs?', *Change*, 29 (1976) pp. 185–98 and 31 (1976) pp. 131–62.
2. Cf., for one example among thousands, Deleuze and Guattari,*Kafka* (Paris,:Seuil, 1975) pp. 43 ff.
3. 'Languages are imperfect because multiple; the supreme language is missing' (Mallarmé, 'Crisis in Poetry', in Bradford Cook (trans.), *Mallarmé: Selected Prose Poems, Essays and Letters* (Baltimore: The Johns Hopkins Press, 1956) p. 38.
4. This is why the grammarian argues from examples which, by definition, involve the repeatable.
5. The manuscript sources of the *Course* are very clear on this point. Cf. the critical edition of Engler, *Le Cours de Linguistique Générale*, (Wiesbaden: O. Harrassowitz, 1967–1974) B 18–25, and that of Tullio de Mauro, *Cours de Linguistique Générale* (Paris: Payot, 1972), pp. 411–12.
6. Conveniently summarised in R. H. Robins, *A Short History of Linguistics* (London:Longmans, 1967) pp. 19–22.
7. (Paris: SEDES,1968) pp. 92–7.
8. Two translations of the *Ars Poetica* in English translate *usus* in terms of 'usage' as opposed to 'need', thus interpreting Horace's text as concerned with *langue* as opposed to *langage*. Thus, the literal interpretation of Jacob Fuchs gives the crucial line as 'use determines this'. See Jacob Fuchs, *Horace's Satires and Epistles* (New York: W. W.

Norton, 1977), p. 86. This interpretation is perhaps even more marked in the freer rendering of Burton Raffel:

> 'Dead words
> >   shall live
> And live words
> >   shall die,
> And only the mouths of men can decide'.

The Essential Horace: Odes, Epodes, Satires, and Epistles (San Francisco: North Point Press, 1983). [Translator's note.]

3

A Subtle and Failing Linguistics

Lalangue is not-all. It follows from this that there is something which does not cease to not be written in it, and in all the discursive forms which are related to *lalangue*, this something exerts its power. For linguistics, it is a simple matter, one which consists in totally ignoring the point of cessation. This act of ignoring that point structures it.

Before making precise what is at stake, I would like to throw some preliminary light on it by considering a completely contrary case, a position which is defined by not ignoring the point of cessation, by unflaggingly returning to it, by never consenting to consider it nothing – in short, poetry. Let us take as given this lack, this want, which marks *lalangue*. If a being is assigned to it, it then becomes understandable how speaking this being, making it cease to not be written, should come to be imposed as a duty. An essential step, to which some will bear witness – Yves Bonnefoy, read in this light, should make clear the sense in which the act of poetry consists in transcribing in *lalangue* itself and through its own proper channels a point of cessation of the failure to be written. It is in this that lies poetry's concern with truth, because truth is, by its very structure, what language is wanting in, and with ethics, because the point of cessation, once encompassed, insists on being spoken.

In any case, there is nothing new in this and it is easy to identify, within the critical tradition, various names for the point of cessation that could be called the point of poetry – for one it is death, for another the obscene, for another the purest meaning that is achieved by extracting words from the sphere of ordinary reference – what is called hermeticism. For another, finally, Mallarmé[1] or Saussure, the point at which lack ceases, a point which,

74

in addition, makes up for it, is located in sound itself, which it becomes a question thus of stripping of what makes it useful for communication, in other words, the distinctive – no longer the highest purity of meaning, but a multi-faceted homophony.

What is amazing is that the failure is not absolute and that poets are recognised by their actually managing, if not to make up for the lack, at least to have some effect on it. In *lalangue*, which they fashion, subjects leave their mark, opening up a route where something impossible to write comes to be written.

This is precisely what linguistics, like grammar, must ignore. That is why the first must take language as an object of science, form and not matter. It is a matter of its very being, as well as of what that presupposes as a way of dealing with the not-all.

For language, as we have claimed, supports the not-all of *lalangue*, but in order for this not-all to be made the object of science, it must be grasped as a *completeness*. Language is the system measured against which *lalangue* is found wanting, lacking. In this way linguistics is 'subtle' in Lacan's sense. Like Kant's consciousness before the universality of the law, it quibbles with the all and the not-all.

In order to succeed, linguistics must simply ignore the lack, the want, and maintain: (1) that for linguistics there is nothing to know about *lalangue* and (2) that the system of the impossible which marks it is consistent and complete. A comparison with grammar will make precise exactly what this involves.

Grammar represents language, but not by a symbolic writing; instead, it constructs an image of it. The requirement of completeness thus takes on an imaginary colouring and is transposed in terms of totality: qualitative totality, that is to say, perfection (this is the reason every grammar is at the same time a praise of the language described) and quantitative totality (this is the reason grammar is only conceived of as complete). The notion of a grammatical fragment is a contradiction in terms, the image of a totality being unable to be anything but total itself. As for language, it acquires the consistence proper to the imaginary and its totality is that of phantasy.

This is why the language of grammarians is shifted so easily towards empty display, the real that constitutes it being converted into a social reality, the badge of prestige. Here we recognise normative grammar, in which the impossible of the not-all barring a subject is grasped as an obligation for an *I*, for an ego.

Linguistic representation is specifically of the order of science. In it, the requirement of completeness thus functions differently, no longer being measured by an external totality, but according to internal criteria. As a result, fragments of linguistics are conceivable and, in truth, that is all that is conceivable. There is no complete linguistics, in the sense that there are complete grammars, but there are complete writings, meant to represent the complete set of the data motivating their symbolism and their formal properties, and not the complete set of what belongs to language. As for consistency, it is the sort which is required of writings, in which the permitted sequences must not be contradictory.

Falling outside of science, grammar does not have to be non-contradictory or homogenous. Consequently, the completeness that it works toward can be obtained by any kind of tinkering. Similarly, the not-all which marks its domain hardly presents it with any difficulties. It is enough for it to make up for the lack with any kind of patchwork. The feeling for language on which, implicitly or not, all grammarians worthy of the name depend thus guarantees them that, whatever their own insufficiency may be, the completeness of language is there, present in each of the subjects who speak it.

On the contrary, the type of writing that linguistics has in view cannot be achieved if the not-all retains the least title to existence. All that remains then is to know nothing about it, to ignore everything that proceeds from *lalangue*. It is obvious then why linguistics, unlike the grammatical tradition, has had difficulties with the mother tongue. We know that the whole effort of structuralist linguists consisted in requiring linguists to treat every language as if no one spoke it, and if it turned out to be their own language, to treat it as a foreign idiom. This was evidently the surest way to prevent any embarrassing return of what could undo or 'discomplete' the object to be represented. The move of transformational grammar is even subtler: in it, in the opposite way, one is only truly in the position to describe one's own language, the surest empirical recourse, when it comes to reconstructing the system of the real, being direct intuition. Hence, one situates within each subject a *dictamen*, the voice of the impossible, as perfect as a moral imperative.

In the real of language a certain knowledge, called 'competence', is assumed and within this knowledge a certain subject, called the 'speaking subject'. Linguists are simply those who write out this competence; but if their own should be the one concerned, it is apparent that their position is not simple – the speaking subject, a point with neither dimension nor desire nor unconscious, is simply cut to the measure of the subject of the enunciation or utterance and is made to mask the latter, or more precisely to suture it; let a linguist so function, and each enouncement[2] or statement that this linguist utters as subject can be at the same time the occasion of an analysis, and vice versa. The mother tongue is thus continuously stripped of its predicate, but in exchange *lalangue* is always in the process of infecting language.

The relation of linguists to their own language is twofold in structure. It is held together at that point where the not-all must be projected into an all. It is thus always in the process of imagining a signifier which would make up for the failure of language and would make language all, a master-word,[3] for instance. The discipline would thus seem to be organised entirely around this word and able by means of it to untie all the knots of Language – singling it out to occupy a position of universal mastery over all discourses, from which it is supposed to be able to empty all want. As for the subject who first utters the master-word, he finds himself by that very act in the position of master and his person alone suffices to bear witness to those who hear him that what is wanting has been made up for.[4]

Here we touch on what links linguistics, considered as a science, to the cabal, in the two senses of this term – there has not been, in the history of this discipline, a period when groups were not formed around a subject supposed to possess the key word, when one could not fail to recognise in it the classic configurations of faithful and unfaithful disciples, of books in secret codes, of the exoteric and the esoteric, and finally of persecution. For it goes without saying that between the different cliques, distinct by virtue of the candidate which they promote in the role of master-word, there is a merciless struggle.

In this sense, linguistics brings to its full realisation the arche-type of those professions Valéry qualifies as 'delirious' – and not without good reason, for the key to this delirium, which Valery describes, but does not explain, lies in the fact that the practi-tioners of these professions are sustained by no real recognisable to any but themselves.[5] Language is thus a real, we insist, but it now must be added, of a nature very peculiar, because the impossible in it never ceases to be misconstrued. To demonstrate it, a deduction was required.[6]

In fact, to accept that an impossible circumscribes language is to be already a linguist or a grammarian. Nothing intervenes to insure this circle, constitutive of the disciplines, and to guarantee for its professionals the existence of that which qualifies them.

No doubt, it would seem that one is able to say the same apropos of all the so-called human sciences: the difference is that the latter have typically to do with realities the constraint of which is properly speaking a *parody* of the impossible – while linguistics makes contact with a real, and it is not in any metaphoric sense or by tinkering that it can claim to formalise it. As a consequence, the circle that can be oberved elsewhere owes more to the hermeneutic tradition. Like the interpreter of the sacred text, the ethnologist, the economist, the psychologist, the sociologist are bound by the conditions of the reality they describe and comment on – whence the trivial relation of uncertainty which unites observer and object of observation. But the circle of linguistics is far different; it is not the result of the conditions of observation, but of the properties of the real of language – and of the 'forgettable' character of its effects.

What is more, however necessary it may be for linguistics to ignore what exceeds the orbit of its own writing, it is not clear that it would have the power to do so. We know that for linguistics the exorbitant is concentrated in a point which it sutures – the subject of the enunciation or utterance. Let us suppose then that in the system of the real segments appear that could not be described without bringing in precisely this subject. In this case, linguistic writing would be divided between two absolute and contradictory imperatives: that of completeness, according to which such segments must receive a representation, and that of consistency, according to which all representation must obey the same laws of writing.

Now such segments do exist; some of them have long been recognised. Damourette and Pichon had already noted the 'expletive' *ne* and certain imperfects, to which one can add many others: expletives, insults, indirect discourse, and so on. In all these cases, one can isolate data of an impossible sort whose explanation must have recourse, no longer to the speaking subject, symmetricisable and non-desiring, but to a subject of the enunciation or utterance, capable of desire and non-symmetricisable. A situation no doubt linguistics can guard against by a few subterfuges to which we will return, but which cannot eliminate the subversion it is subject to.

From this point on, the systems of the real to which linguistics is tied are revealed to lay out routes which either go nowhere, or become lost in the forest of *lalangue*. There are only two alternatives: either one can opt for the ethic of science, wanting to know nothing about that point where the path becomes lost. This is the position of transformational grammar. Or one can opt for the ethic of the ethic of truth, where one must, as linguist, and in the very writing one is restricted to, articulate that point, not as indistinguishable, but as capable of being signalled via the failing it imposes on all guidelines and signals.

Notes

1. '[Verse] atones for the sins of languages', Mallarmé, 'Crisis in Poetry', in Bradford Cook (trans.), *Mallarmé* (Baltimore: The Johns Hopkins Press, 1956) p. 38.
2. Here I follow Samuel Beckett in translating *énoncé* as *enouncement*. [Translator's note.]
3. The history of linguistics can be summed up in a series of such master-words: the exceptionlessness of phonetic laws, the arbitrariness of the sign, structure, transformation, are the most well-known examples. Along parallel lines, one could describe a series of cliques gathered around a subject uttering the master-word.
4. By that he also bears witness, *qua* subject, that the integral knowledge of language is possible. In other words, he is the subject supposed to know. But this is not analytic discourse, where the analyst maintains his position in abjectness and silence. The problem for the possessor of the master-word is that he speaks, and what is more, speaks in the territory of science, where all claims can be measured. He is thus necessarily condemned to demonstrating just what is impossible in subjectivising the position of the subject supposed to know, by uttering at least one proposition which devalues him and makes him the subject supposed to be in ignorance, to not know. The master in linguistics, as in all science, is then suddenly also he who produces a foolish statement – all others declaring themselves disciples by locating it where they see fit.
5. The reference is to the following passage from Valéry: 'Paris contains and combines, and consummates and consumes, most of the brilliant failures summoned by their destinies to the *delirious professions* . . . By this I mean all those occupations in which the principal instrument is one's opinion of oneself, and the raw material is the opinion of you held by others. The persons who practice them, and so are committed to being perennial candidates, are necessarily always afflicted with

certain delusions of grandeur, endlessly crossed and tormented by delusions of persecution. This tribe of *uniques* is ruled by the law of the *best* – that is, of those who have the pluck to will something obviously absurd . . . They live for nothing else but to achieve the last illusion of being alone – for superiority is merely a solitude situated at the present limits of a species. Each of them founds his own existence on the nonexistence of others, who must be forced however to agree that they do not exist' (Valéry's ellipses).

In Paul Valéry, *Monsieur Teste,* Jackson Matthews (trans.), in *The Collected Works of Paul Valéry*, vol. 6 (Princeton: Princeton University Press, 1973) pp. 50–1.

Lacan cites the passage in his thesis *De la Psychose Paranoïaque dans ses Rapports avec la Personnalité suivi de Premiers Ecrits sur la Paranoïa,* (Paris: Seuil, 1978) p. 278, and again in 'Situation de la Psychanalyse en 1956', *Ecrits* (Paris: Seuil, 1966) p. 479 and footnote. [Translator's note.]

6. It is in this sense, perhaps, that Saussure said that the units of language did not present themselves to immediate observation.

4

A Single and Indivisible Linguistics

We have been speaking of 'linguistics', thereby presupposing the uniqueness of the referent of the word. Nevertheless, it would be easy to show that extremely diverse theories lay claim to this title, and not unjustifiably, differing on what should be understood by theory, by science, by demonstration, and so on. If we want the term 'linguistics' to function as something other than an administrative rubric, we must try to determine whether there is a common core for all its existing versions, a core which could become from then on the referent of the term in question.

If we take into account the development of this discipline, the task will take on a simple form, coming down to the resolution of the following question: what are the theses common to structuralist grammars and transformational grammars?

It is a fact that linguistics has been dominated in an overwhelming fashion by a reference to structuralism, and it is also a fact that this domination is at present a thing of the past. Structuralism is best taken here as something precise and not as the somewhat pedestrian vision of the world or the general, rather simple epistemology that is usually designated by this name, but a set of non-trivial propositions bearing on the real of language and the form of its representation. They can be summarised in the following manner:

– linguistics is scientific if, and only if, it defines language as a system of signs;
– all the operations necessary to the science must be deduced from this principle, and only the operations deduced from this principle are acceptable as part of science.

None of these propositions is self-evident in any of its parts. Transformational grammar, in particular, denies them, assuming entirely different properties for language not reducible to any type of sign system.

For a long time, nonetheless, the notion of linguistics appeared to be coextensive with its structuralist version; and today still, it is readily supposed that, regardless of extensions and modifications, linguistics needs the notion of the sign.[1]

This consubstantial union of linguistics and the sign is invested with a unique authority, and one essentially unquestioned: Saussure's *Course in General Linguistics*. To such an extent that structuralism, as it is understood here, comes down to this assertion: all linguistics is by definition Saussurian. At the same time, the question that we raised at the start can be transposed into the following one: what is left today of Saussure?

Saussure's position can be appreciated at this point through the combination of three guidelines. The first is none other than the ideal of science, which, in the *Course*, is stated in the Language of foundations – what is at stake is the founding of linguistics as a science.

This goal, once acknowledged, has not gone without generating certain misunderstandings, and particularly in drawing, in modern thinking, an undue parallel with Freud. Yet, one thing should be made clear – Freud is an innovator. When he established foundations, he caused to come into existence a hitherto unprecedented configuration. As for Saussure, this was not at all the case – for him, linguistics already existed, namely, comparative grammar. The problem was that it was not cognisant of what rendered it possible.

It is not a question of beginning, but of legitimating – here we recognise the Kantian mode. And the answers that Saussure offered are, also, in this mode. For linguistics as a science to be possible, one must, he would say, distinguish phenomena from things in themselves. In this manner, one obtains a series of pairs, certain of which are celebrated:

Things in themselves	Phenomena
Language (*le langage*)	language (*la langue*)
sound as a sonorous continuum	sound as segment or phoneme or signifier
the idea or the sense	the signified
the connection between a sound and a thing in the world	the arbitrariness of the sign

Even the caveat of the transcendental dialectic can be found, and in the very same terms, in Saussure: if linguistics claims to go to things in themselves, it falls into antinomies; and, rather than to the *Antinomies linguistiques* of Victor Henry, it is in fact to those of Kant that we must refer the Saussurian antinomies.

The linguistics which here exists and whose foundations are at stake is comparative grammar, the only discipline which, furthermore, Saussure practised. Only, in the process of setting forth its general conditions, Saussure discovered that it was not the sole form of scientific linguistics possible. In other words, the concepts of *language*, of the *sign*, of *difference*, and so on needed to give an account of the reconstruction of Indo-European are found to have a more general application and to justify other approaches. This is, furthermore, what could have given the impression that Saussure was instituting a new science; but it is easy to see the extent to which this is an illusion. It should be made clear, from the conceptual point of view, that there is nothing in post-Saussurian synchronic linguistics – essentially Troubetzkoy's phonology – which is not already in comparative grammar.

In the Kantian Language of foundations, one easily recognises the pure and simple affirmation of the ideal of science. In constructing the principles by which linguistics could be legitimised, Saussure thought only to accomplish one thing: to range within science every proposition that he stated *qua* linguist. Science then becomes the ideal point at which all of these propositions intersect, symbolic agency by which its discourse is organised.

But science itself must be made representable – that is to say, must give rise to some consistent theory. By this same move, the ideal of science, as symbolic agency, is refracted in its imaginary correlate: an ideal science, which to all intents and purposes embodies it. In this manner a second guideline for deciding Saussure's position is defined: given that he sought to legitimate a science, one must add that he referred it implicitly to a bundle of distinctive features permitting him to recognise its ideal form.

In other words, a particular model of science: in short, let us call it Euclidean.[2] Following this model, a science is a discourse governed by two principles:

- the principle of the minimum: all the concepts of the science must be deduced from a minimum number of axioms, expressed in a minimum number of primitive concepts;
- the principle of the self-evident: all the axioms and primitive concepts must be evident, which exempts them from having to be demonstrated or defined.

In the third place, Saussure selects a privileged concept which allows him to articulate the relation of the ideal of science to the ideal science, the enterprise of foundations and the Euclidean model: the *sign*. Thanks to it, one possesses an unerring rule for delimiting the jurisdiction of phenomena: in the set of things in themselves gravitating within the orbit of Language, only the features that can be attributed to the sign are brought into focus out of a possible observation – the semiological, to invoke Saussure's term, which thus takes on its true value. But in addition, the sign makes possible the construction of linguistic science in absolute conformity with the prevailing model:

(a) there is *one* axiom, the absolute minimum, and it is evident: 'language is a system of signs';
(b) there is *one* primitive concept, and it is evident: the concept of the sign.

From this axiom which rests undemonstrated and with the aid of this concept which remains undefined,[3] all the operations necessary to linguistics can be derived – but it is not true that only linguistic operations are deducible. In substituting for 'language' another term, an infinity of self-evident axioms is obtained, all capable of founding a science. This is why, all too logically, Saussure talks of a general semiology, implicitly replacing the initial axiom by a schema of the type: '''*X* is a system of signs', *X* being capable of receiving as its value practically any well-defined domain of objects.

With the non-Saussurians, each of the three guidelines – the ideal of science, the ideal science, the sign – leads to refinements and modifications. The first is, in fact, maintained, not perhaps in its Kantian form, but in its essentials, as follows: all the forms of linguistics, including transformational grammar, are organised according to the ideal of science and for the construction of their own knowledge single out objects which they wish to know nothing about–an operation equivalent to the distinction between phenomena and things in themselves.[4] Its principle, moreover, will become apparent to us. It is the twisting and turning of the all and the not-all to which linguistics is tied. Whether *langue* is apprehended as a phenomena of *langage* or as a way of treating the not-all of *lalangue* is in this respect immaterial; or rather the second moment is the truth of the first.

In contradistinction to the ideal of science, the guideline of the ideal science has totally changed its form today; for transformational grammar in particular, the model is certainly not of the Euclidean type. For the axioms and principles of the self-evident and of the minimum, it substitutes hypotheses, the non-self-evident and the maximum, the more highly valued theory being the one involving the greatest number of falsifiable (hence non-evident) hypotheses. In effect, the ideal science has become Popperian.[5]

Insofar as the concept of the sign articulates both the first two guidelines, the role it plays is necessarily affected by the disappearance of the Euclidean model. In this sense, the sign constitutes a critical point of this investigation – it makes it possible to measure what, in Saussure, is linked to a particular conception of science, and what falls outside this conception. By a kind of concomitant variation, it will thus be possible to isolate what is invariable, the candidate for representing the nucleus of every possible linguistics.

Let us thus consider the Saussurian theory of the sign. Many others have done so, though none seem to have raised the question as to whether such a theory actually exists. After all, as has often been noted, Saussure is not the first to have recourse to the term and the concept. Indeed, it is a commonplace of the philosophical tradition, at least since the Stoics, to refer the actual givens of language to it.[6] Now, if this tradition is examined with attention, a crucial feature of it should become apparent: the theory of the sign is always a theory of the plurality of types of signs – conventional, natural, accidental, and so on. And this is indeed the theory of the sign, that is to say a theory having the sign as its *object*. In such a theory, Language, insofar as it is ascribed to a particular type of sign, is inserted in a broader classification, one of whose areas it illustrates.

In Saussure, on the contrary, there is only one type; in this sense, the sign is not the object of a theory, but the *means* by which to set forth a theory whose object is something entirely different. It so happens in actual fact that the properties attributed by Saussure recapitulate more or less precisely those that tradition assigns to one of the types that it distinguishes – in such a manner that it is not difficult to find echoes of the *Course* in Saint Augustine or Condillac – but it should be stated plainly, such echoes are without interest; between the configurations, in which the signs are lined up according to various types, in which the diverse relations which unite their two sides are worked out in detail, and the one in which the Unique and its unvarying properties are bluntly posited, there can be nothing in common – or, to take up an old structuralist line of argument, between an element x apprehended in a system in which it is opposed to y and z and the 'same' x which is opposed to nothing, there is no identity.

The object of Saussurian theory is linguistics itself, and the concept of the sign is its expression, indeed borrowed from a tradition; it is not evident that such an expression is necessary; it is also not evident, even if this expression is adequate, that the properties of the sign which lend it to expressing the object in view do anything more than encounter by chance the very thing which is at stake. Such is indeed the itinerary of Saussure, but no doubt he was unaware of it himself – the philosophical tradition offered him a concept, he made it his own when the occasion arose.

The sign, unique of its kind, has in Saussure three properties which are given as needing no explanation and calling for no empirical proof nor rational demonstration – it is arbitrary, negative, two-sided. It is to be remarked that of these three properties the last is contained in the concept of the sign itself, and for this reason, I need scarcely return to it;[7] the other two, on the contrary, are not self-evident, and perhaps Saussure claims them for the *linguistic* sign only, to the exclusion of any other.

(a) The Arbitrary

I will not reconsider in detail the criticism of this term, which Lacan has shown marked the hold of the discourse of the Master, as if Saussure could recognise a law in language only by conjuring up the figure of a legislator – if only to obliterate it. Instead, I would like to establish what this concept accomplishes.

It has in fact two roles, one positive, the other negative. The first comes down to positing that language is subject to the law of an absolute *dualism*. In other words, there exist two orders, that of signs and that of things, nothing of the first being able to act as a cause for the second and vice versa. From which it follows that between the sign and the thing signified, the relation is that of a simple chance meeting.

But one must go further: sound also belongs as such to the order of things, and likewise the idea or the signified, so that, in accordance with this dualism, the linkage which groups them together in their capacity as things can have nothing in common with the linkage which groups them together in their capacity as sides of a sign – no cause arising from the first can operate on the second. Arbitrariness thus governs not only the relation of the thing signified to the sign, but also that of the signifier to the signified – contrary to what Benveniste maintained in a celebrated article[8].

The arbitrary, in this sense, only names the encounter – what Lacan better names contingence, and also what Mallarmé names Chance.[9] In locating it at the heart of language, Saussure is empowered to construct a theory of signs which in no way involves a theory of things. Henceforth, linguistics is no longer a vision of the world, and the link which united it from the time of the Greeks to the theory of the being of things is severed.[10]

This amounts to saying that through the arbitrary, linguistics is put in the position of not knowing. At this point one meets again the second, negative function of the concept.

That a particular sound refers to a particular sense, that a particular sign refers to a particular thing, is now thought of as a purely accidental occurrence – why it should be like that rather

For the Love of Language

than otherwise the arbitrary says that there is no way of knowing. More precisely, the arbitrariness of the sign comes down to positing that it cannot be thought of as other than it is, since there is no reason for its being like it is. The arbitrary is perfectly tailored to cover over a question which will never be asked: what is the sign when it is not the sign? what is language before it is language? – let us say the question that is usually expressed in terms of origins. To say that the sign is arbitrary is to posit as a primitive thesis: *there is language.*[11]

(b) The Negative

The linguistic sign is negative, that is to say, following Saussure, oppositional and relative.

This means two things: first of all that the signs are several and arranged in order. Within this order, each sign has identity only through the relation that it maintains with the others (together and separately). Here one again finds a dualism, all that could confer on a sign an independent identity being attributed to the order of things, and for this reason ignored. Whence it also follows that only a single type of relation can be defined, for everything which could vary them in some other way is eliminated from attention – between a sign *a* and a sign *b*, since one cannot say what *a* or *b* is separately, one can simply say that one is not the other and vice-versa. This is called an opposition.

Secondly, negativity implies that the linguistic units are not given to immediate intuition. Since these units are signs, according to Saussure, they cannot receive identity except through the system of relations of their order: hence, they can only be deduced.

(c) Two-Sidedness

On the subject of this property, there is scarcely anything to say except the following: it makes it possible to consider in terms of the sign a property recognised from time immemorial in Language, the relation between a sonorous movement, a vibration of the air, and a meaning, idea, concept, and so on.

As can be seen, these three properties are very different and their interconnection is not evident. And yet, it is by having brought them together into a single point and having called this point 'sign' that Saussure gave his doctrines their singular features. There is no reason one cannot conceive of a theory *T* where all three continue to exist, but differently distributed. In that case, the concept of the sign vanishes, without moreover there being incompatibility between *T* and the *Course*.

To be accurate, dualism is only a particular form of the operation which deals with the not-all, and of its counterpart: ignorance. It must be made clear: every linguistic theory has to pass via this route, and we know why this is so. Every science, of which linguistics is here only one case, is the construction of a writing and is defined as a science in that it allows no writing that is not a writing of the repeatable. Which implies that it equally sets aside what, in reality, is not necessary to the repetition in its object, as what in itself is not repeatable – the accidental, shall we say – as finally what could, in what is repeated, mask what is there repeated, for example individual variations. The arbitrary sign in Saussure is what mediates all exclusions at one stroke; another linguistics, differently grounded, transformational grammar, for example, can arrive at the same results by completely different routes: the explicit exclusion of certain data, 'memory limitations, distractions, shifts of attention and interest, and errors'(*Aspects*, p. 3); but moreover also, by pure and simple silence blanketing everything which could play the part of a thing in the world, alien to the repetition of examples: social reality, anthropology, psychology, and so on. The only difference from the *Course* is that the concept of the sign does not underlie the operation and, consequently, that no specific property, such as the arbitrary, has to call attention to it. A kind of protocol thus suffices, stated at the outset of the theory, and which is never returned to, or even merely a zone of silence, invisibly encircling its domain.

The thesis of negativity was divided into two sub-theses: one impinged on the analysis of the concept of the sign, the other on the nature of the linguistic units. For convenience's sake, I will for the moment examine only the second, postponing the first till later. That the units of linguistics are not given to immediate intuition is ultimately a question of fact, susceptible to empirical examination and not just to nominal definitions. But this is to say at the same time that differences of principle would not necessarily be at stake if some linguistic theory, unlike the *Course*, took the position that the units are immediate.

Now such is indeed the case: implicitly or not, all structuralist grammars have actually proceeded as if their units had to be constructed; for transformational grammar, on the contrary, the set of operations of construction – the establishment of distributions, of oppositions, of paradigms, etc. – is irrelevant. The units are given; the task is simply to describe them.[12] No doubt this involves great empirical differences between the two types of theory; one cannot maintain, however, that they make impossible the isolation of a common core.

That the sign is two-sided is implied in the very notion of the sign, yet it is nevertheless the case that Language lends itself to being so represented. For Saussure, and for many others before him, this possibility is a matter of course; but let us suppose that we uncouple the relation of Language to the sign. What remains to be explained is how it comes to seem so self-evident. This is due to the fact that we cannot think of Language without pairing a sonorous vibration and something else, the absent, the idea, the sense. It is this pure difference, which furthermore destines Language and philosophy for one another, which the sign makes it possible to capture and to fix so that it becomes susceptible of treatment. No doubt, this susceptibility to treatment is essential to linguistics and linguistics ought to try to guarantee it; but here again, it is not obvious that the sign is the only means to do this which it has at its disposal. Let us once more consider transformational grammar. Pure difference has its place in it and is rendered perfectly representable by the simple position of levels in the theory – one called phonological, the other semantic. Their presence and their definition appear then as a general condition of the good construction of theories. Instead of a specific concept – that of the sign – it is the form of the theory which expresses the pure difference at the heart of Language.

It is already apparent in what sense the very properties whose combination constitutes the Saussurean sign can be maintained for the most part, except precisely in their combination. The only one left is the most peculiar: negativity understood in its non-empirical sense. It is here that superficially linguistics is most closely bound to its structuralist version. And yet, reduced to its essentials, the thesis says only this: *in language, there exists the discernible.*

Or, to put it once more in Lacan's terms, in language there exists the One. In Saussure, we have seen, the sign is the device by means of which the object is divided up into squares in the name of the discernment which it renders possible; in Chomsky, a similar device is at work, under the form of an affirmation: for each level of the grammar, there are minimal units (cf. *Aspects*, pp. 179–80, n. 2). In both cases, what is involved is the same thing – rendering a writing possible.

To summarise: in the first place, far from the theory of the sign being in any way essential to linguistics, it is doubtful that linguistics has ever constructed one. In the second place, if one correctly analyses the concept of the sign, it appears that its properties can be perfectly well preserved by other means, the core of linguistics being then composed of three elements, in various combinations, depending on the model:

- the choice of a model of science – the model can vary, but not the demand for there to be one; this implies in any case that the object must be made representable, that is to say, regular;
- the operation which deals with the not-all, where the will not to know is exerted, and brings about regularisation;
- the thesis of the discernible.

Up till now, our point of view has been strictly epistemological: an ordering, classification and differentiation of concepts. As always, this sort of enterprise bears within itself its own limits and we have reached them. The point which reveals it is precisely the thesis of the discernible.

As we have presented it, this thesis is essentially indistinguisable from the the fact that linguistics imposes on an object which is unaware of them the networks of discernment which are appropriate to it. In other words, at the beginning there is a stream into which are inserted cuts, which have in themselves no title to being thought of as real – a nominalist thesis, current, implicitly or not, with the structuralists.

Now, this is not what is required for linguistics. Such a way of presenting the issues might be suitable for history, for sociology, for the various hermeneutic disciplines; but unlike them, linguistics is directed at a *real*, and it is this real that it requires be marked by the discernible, the One. It is not its writing which establishes the One by convention, but on the contrary it is the latter which makes this writing possible. It is not on the level of the object of linguistics, as such, that the discernible is established, but on the level of what renders it possible: not on the level of language, but on that of *lalangue*.

Here, one touches on the essence of what, in linguistics, is of interest to psychoanalysis. Reduced to the minimum, the Freudian thesis could be stated in the following way: the fact that there is language has to do with the fact that there is an unconscious, whence it follows that the mechanisms of the first repeat those of the second (this is the claim about the antithetical sense of primal words) and vice-versa. Whence it follows more precisely that a point can be defined where language – at one and the same time the fact that there is such a thing, and the fact that it has such and such a form – and unconscious desire are articulated. This point, Lacan, unlike Freud, has named: it is *lalangue* – or, what comes down to the same concept, the speaking being, the *parlêtre*.

What linguistics attests to, by its mere possibility, is that this point where language and desire are mutually corrupted by one another is not to be represented as a stream, but consists in a signifying articulation. It is by that alone that its writing makes contact with a real. Moreover, in this sense, linguistics says nothing more than the slip of the tongue and the verbal joke, which however it musters all its willpower to turn away from; for them too it is *lalangue* and the One which are presupposed.

For this reason, for Lacan, as for Freud before him, it is not a particular form of linguistics which matters – structuralist any more than transformational, synchronic any more than diachronic – but the mere fact that, in the case of language, something of the order of a writing is possible. For Freud, Abel's somewhat dubious comparative grammar sufficed; Lacan is more demanding, but when it comes down to it scarcely much more – for him, it is not even necessary for linguistics, provided it exists to its own satisfaction, to be fully aware of its own methods.

And after all, is it so crucial for psychoanalysis for linguistics in the strict sense to be possible and to go on existing on its own? For, all things considered, the thesis of the discernible in no way distinguishes linguistics as such from grammar – where the two disciplines diverge is in their treatment of the not-all and in their reference to science. But this is precisely what is of so little importance for psychoanalysis. Only the 'there is a One in *lalangue*' counts for it; and since the dawn of time, from the instant when the first man said 'That is correct', this is what grammar has presupposed.

Lalangue is not a continuum, on which by cuts the One is imposed, and language is not reducible to a territorialisation carried out with knowledge in view. This is already what the verbal joke, the slip of the tongue, free associations, attest to – in a word, the pure possibility of psychoanalytic listening. It is also what invests grammar and linguistics with their authority. Not that they have anything to do with *lalangue*, but rather with something which only its existence makes possible. What is more, they do not even have anything properly to do with signifiers, since the subject that these would represent they are unaware of, but the arguments that they construct, writing out a real, are ever on the point of toppling into signifying chains. For this it suffices to refer them to their cause: the One structuring *lalangue*.

Psychoanalysis, then, is supported by what linguistics and grammar presuppose, and what these latter guarantee by their success. However, linguistics, as a science, could vanish, and the support that psychoanalysis derives from it not disappear, since it depends in no way on the demand of being integrated into science – all that matters is simply the possibility of a writing.

This possibility alone is in no way trivial – when it comes to Language, no philosophy has ever invoked it. The step which the grammarian has achieved and which the linguist has perfected is, in this respect, of singularly far-reaching significance. In truth, everything in everyday experience goes against the idea that for objects as intimately connected to reality as words, one could construct a writing owing precisely nothing to this reality. More-over, the agency of the One thus takes on a new form – from time immemorial, philosophy had recognised it in nature, as the locus of the *stoicheia*, to the point of summoning these up in the figure of the world and their integral knowledge in the figure of God. With grammar, and its intersection with science – linguistics – the One appears not only outside of nature, but in the very thing one would have wished to define by this externality. Galileo's small letters are revealed as capable of spelling out something other than the *physis*, or rather the other of the *physis*. A fissure is thus opened in the figure of the world, insofar as it could claim to be coextensive with the reign of the One; a new mode of being emerges, that of a non-physical One, which Saussure exhausted himself in delineating, and the structuralists after him.

The advance of psychoanalysis, and perhaps it would not have been possible without the construction of linguistic writing (if only under the form as yet veiled of comparative grammar), is to have recognised in this new mode of being unconscious processes.[13] In this very precise sense, one can continue to maintain for linguistics a privilege, which the course it has followed has as its property to make it neglect.

Notes

1. See, for example, J.-L. Nancy and P. Lacoue-Labarthe, *Le Titre de la lettre* (Paris: Galilée, 1973) p. 41, where they speak of 'this impossibility: a linguistics without a theory of the sign'.
2. It is obviously Aristotle who established its theory; it can be summed up more fully in the following terms:

   A. An Aristotelian science is a series of propositions bearing on the elements of one and the same domain, and presenting the following properties:

   (1) the propositions of this series are divided into axioms and derived propositions (theorems);
   (2) the concepts appearing in the propositions of the series are divided into primitive concepts and derived concepts.

   B. Of the axioms, the following is required:

   (1) they must be self-evident and by this fact undemonstrable;
   (2) they must be sufficient, in the sense that in addition to them, only the rules of logic are needed to demonstrate a theorem.

   C. Of the primitive concepts, the following is required:

   (1) they must be immediately intelligible and by reason of this undefinable;
   (2) they must be sufficient, in the sense that in addition to them, only certain operations of combination are necessary to construct the derived concepts.

   The source of this presentation is Scholz, 'Die Axiomatik der Alten',*Mathesis Universalis* (Basle: Schwabe, 1969) pp. 27–44. Cf. also my own *Arguments Linguistiques* (Paris: Mame, 1973). The Euclidean model is practically the only one, until recently, to have been recognised by philosophy; it is hence not very surprising that Saussure should have taken his inspiration from it. The principle of the self-evident is explicitly affirmed by all commentators. The same cannot be said for the principle of the minimum, which arises nevertheless out of the constant *practice* of those who comment upon the sciences.

3. Everything that passes with Saussure as a definition of the sign (*Course in General Linguistics*, New York: McGraw-Hill, pp. 66–7) concerns only in fact the property specific to the linguistic sign, namely what distinguishes it insofar as *linguistic*. But nothing is said of the concept itself ot the *sign*, whose content comes down to the most impoverished of notions: a pure and simple association and a pure and simple difference. It would be misplaced, however, to fault Saussure with this; on the contrary, it is perfectly justified that a primitive rest in itself undefined.

This in no way weakens its effectiveness – one could easily show that the operations of segmentation and of substitution (usually combined in commutation) are analytically contained in the concept of the Saussurian sign. In fact, they are limited to converting into procedures the relations of association between the two sides and of difference between the signs. Moreover, the correspondence between operations and relations which serve to define the sign has been meticulously made explicit by Benveniste in 'The Levels of Linguistic Analysis', *Problems in General Linguistics*, Mary Elizabeth Meck (trans.), (Coral Gables, Fla.: University of Miami Press, 1971) pp. 101–11.

The reader will see clearly in this text that structuralist descriptions are capable of being wholly derived from a theory governed by the principle of the minimum.

4. Ordinarily, these objects are credited to the variable and the accidental: slips of the tongue, individual tics, failures of attention, and so on, so that the phenomenal is also the regular, and the exclusions seem linked to the very requirements of generalisation. But this misses the point: the opposition *langue/langage*, which arises on the whole from the relation of the phenomenon to the thing in itself, and the opposition *langue/parole*, which arises on the whole from the relation of the regular to the accidental, come down in fact to the same operation.

5. See, of course, Popper's *The Logic of Scientific Discovery* (New York: Basic Books, 1959); cf. also the first chapter of Chomsky's *Aspects of the Theory of Syntax* (Cambridge, Mass.: MIT Press, 1965) and supplementarily my own *Arguments Linguistiques*.

6. It seems in fact that, in Aristotle, the concept of the sign indicates only a type of inference: that which draws a conclusion from a sense datum to an element outside the range of the senses. It is in this way that the sign functions in the Stoics and the Epicureans. True, it is the case that Language is mentioned as an example of inference from the sign, but this in no way amounts to proposing a doctrine of Language; on the contrary, it is the sign which is explained by the supposedly facile illustration of it the word constitutes.

According to R. A. Markus ('Saint Augustine on Signs', in *Augustine*, New York: Doubleday Anchor Books, 1972, pp. 61–91), Saint Augustine turns out to be the first to reverse the relation and put the sign in the service of a theory of Language; from him and not from the Greeks would thus derive all subsequent theories (but see for another, contrary, position B. Darrell Jackson, 'The Theory of Signs in Saint Augustine's *De doctrina christiana*', in R. A. Markus, *Augustine*, pp. 92–147).

   T. Todorov can profitably be consulted, *Théories du symbole* (Paris: Seuil, 1978) pp. 43–58.

7. The only peculiarity of the linguistic sign derives, from this point of view, from the nature of its two sides: the phenomenon of the sound, or signifier, on the one hand, the phenomenon of the sense, or signified, on the other.

8. 'The Sign' in *Problems in General Linguistics*; 'Nature du Signe Linguistique', *Problèmes de Linguistique Générale* (Paris, Gallimard, 1966), pp. 9–55. It should be noted that the postulate is highly improbable if one confines oneself to sense intuition. Who would believe that things cannot act as causes for language, or vice-versa, that language is not a cause in the order of things? But indeed, the arbitrary aims at uprooting linguistics from the verisimilitude of sense impressions. One should recall here Koyré's theses on Galilean physics. [See fn. 26 of translator's introduction.]

9. '[C]hance (which might still have governed these elements, despite their artful and alternating renewal through meaning and sound) is thereby instantly and thoroughly abolished'. Mallarmé, 'Crisis in Poetry', in Bradford Cook (trans.) *Mallarmé: Selected Prose, Poems, Essays and Letters* (Baltimore: The Johns Hopkins Press, 1956) p. 43, from which it follows that the *Coup de Dés* is a proposition about language with a small *l*.

   It would be false to believe that Mallarmé's Chance and Lacan's contingence were simply better names for the arbitrary: the difference in the terms covers over a subversion of the positions. In Saussure, 'arbitrary' means simply the refusal of knowledge; in Mallarmé as in Lacan, the terms are positive and state that a knowledge is possible.

10. Language, in Saussure's sense, belongs to the order of things if one considers its matter; it is from the point of view of its form that it can be disconnected from it. In order for this dualism to have weight, it is thus necessary to consider only form – whence the thesis: language is a form and not a substance.

11. Here again, the misconceptions are frequent – the thesis of the arbitrary has for its function the elimination of any question of origins. It has hence only a superficial resemblance to conventionalism. It is in no way helpful to evoke apropos of the *Course* the opposition of the Greeks *thesei/phusei*, which is a statement about origins, and bears, not on *langue*, but on *langage*.

12. To which one must add, of course, that the units are not of the same type. Thus, in transformational syntax, the unit is the sentence; in structuralist grammars, the sentence can never have this status. The difference is more ancient than it would seem – it is already mentioned, in embryonic form, in the *Course*, pp. 105–7.

13. This is the real significance of the text, so misunderstood by the most eminent, on the contrary meaning contained in primal words. It attests to the fact that Freud himself, however disposed he might have been to recognise as the One only the physical One, had come upon something else.

5

A Detour through the Twists and Turns of the All

'Not all can be said' can be understood in many ways; essentially, it is the proposition which gives shape to the real exactly as linguists encounter it, and which they venture to translate: 'some grammatical construction, marked as incorrect, is excluded'. But that all may not be said is also what designates *another* real, which the linguist as such has nothing to do with: there is something for which words are always wanting, or, there is something impossible to say. Putting them together, as does the French language itself, these two readings get knotted in a difficulty – what for the speaking being is the site of the impossible is also the site of a prohibition.

Not that language furnishes the only evidence for it; on the contrary, in this it only repeats the sexual. Impossible, the sexual relation is for that very reason encased in defences. Whence arises a question: is the prohibition in general connected to the impossible? And is the prohibition which weighs upon grammatical constructions and from which linguists derive their authority related to the loss for words?

But this all which in more than one sense cannot be said we name nevertheless; language proposes with this end in mind signifiers which we do not hesitate to use. It is indeed in this way that we obtain those universalising propositions which, by displaying a mark of the signifier of the All in a point of their course, set themselves off and become valid for some all via some indirect route. But, on the basis of what do we maintain that, for these signifiers of the All, the interpretation must be univocal? on the basis of what are we assured that the universalising propositions are always legitimate, with no other condition than their well-formedness?

It is thus in every sense that the connection of the all to the spoken is of interest to linguistics – insofar as linguistics specifies its object out of the fact that all may not be said – insofar as, out of this very point, it constitutes an all, a whole, moving logically from the fact that everything may not be said to the all of what is said – in so far, finally, as from this all, it intends to say all, by universalising propositions. Linguistics, in short, in its relationship with the spoken, demands the All, in every sense, that is to say, in contradictory senses and by twists and turns. From this, its antinomies are born, and its sophistry, which only become one with its subtlety and its subterfuges. No hope of unravelling them except by confronting the all that one is aiming for in what one says of what is said, with the all of which one says that it is not said.

Grammar and linguistics produce universalising propositions about language. Not that all are universal in the usual sense; it is not difficult to cite ones which are particular or even singular. But even those which enunciate some irreducible exception are meant to hold for every regular case, for every speaking subject defined according to the accepted criteria. In fact, it is really this which is authorised by the operation which delineates language against the backdrop of *lalangue* and isolates the former from the latter – a continuously legitimate usage of the universal operator at some point in the propositions produced about language.

In this way, it can be seen how closely related the operation of language, of *langue*, is to that of Language, of *langage*, the only difference separating them being that of the collective with respect to the distributive: the point of view of Language readily accommodates the universal by the extension and the positioning of the properties common to the various languages, grouping them collectively together into *one* all – language with a small *l*, on the contrary, presupposes the universal distributed over each, in such a way that the universalising propositions are possible for one language among others, even if it is the only one in existence. One and the other points of view, if their respective provinces can even be distinguished, consist then in continuously conjoining to the bits and pieces of the real which present themselves an operator of the All–whether this be the all of classes of words, that of the rule, or at the very least that of the supposed universalisable support of language–the speaking subject.

It is this All, undoubtedly which, in the general opinion, authorises linguistics to its claim to be a science because, since Aristotle, science is connected to the All – is not the *episteme* a set of propositions such that, for an object itself well defined as a whole, an all, they say all, in terms valid for all in all circumstances? For which Galileo seems to change little, the science he founds identifying itself as modern in giving to its object the form of the Universe, and in validating only an all-powerful technique. After all, does not what is essential to any methodology consist simply in delineating the possible modes of constructing a universalising proposition – that is, in showing how the All comes to the bits and pieces. Opinions diverge here, but this is insignificant compared to the concern which unites them. Yet, it is apparent enough that they cannot fail not to arrive at what is essential in science. For, despite appearances, science, in and of itself, has nothing to do with the All. It is achieved only through the constructions of a writing, and the Universe that it is meant to describe or govern is its imaginary recompense – the vain hope that the writings will combine and finally take on a meaning for someone – universal subject or Humanity. But epistemologists do not give up, and each of them is bent on delineating in various ways the recoveries of an All that is held to be the only acceptable guarantee of scientificity.

It would, however, be more profitable to raise questions about foundations and to ask what conditions are necessary for this All, always required and therefore always assumed to be legitimate to be actually legitimate in the order of the signifier – whence, in other words, a proposition is uttered which, universal or particular, is universalised in positing at some point, in its object or in its type of validation, an All. There does not seem to have been much questioning on this point, everyone being too preoccupied with verifying the ways which give entry to the universal, to suspect this universal itself, and to entertain the possibility that this point which it was the goal to arrive at may not always be constructible. It does not seem, in other words, to have been perceived that, whether universal or particular, certain propositions are grouped together on the basis of assuming precisely this: 'some All can be said'. Still less has it been recognised that this assumption itself requires a support which may not be forthcoming.

This is on the contrary what has not escaped Lacan, bringing to light as he did in *l'Etourdit* the cardinal hypothesis of the All – in order for any All to be said, a limit is needed which, in suspending it, would guarantee it as an All constructible in a predeterminate way. This limit is most classically proposed as an existence – at least one – itself constructible, such that it 'says no' to the property defining the All. Supposing then that every use of the All is symbolized under the canonical form $\forall$x. ϕx, this scrap of writing is only sustained by another, the continuous possibility of which it calls forth: $\exists$x. ϕx, an x exists such that for it the All is suspended – limit or exception, that is to say, confirmation.

This, then, is the real of writing. Whether or not for the existence thereby constructed there corresponds a *reality* is not then essential; the important thing is that it can be constructed. Suppose, on the other hand, not that one deny that a reality answers to this existence constructed as a limit, but indeed that this existence may not be constructible – which is written $\overline{\exists}$x. ϕx, 'there does not exist an x which may say no to ϕx' – then, the All is no longer in its turn constructible. No limit suspends it from then on out, nor establishes its domain. From the all of the universe, it seeps out into the all beyond the universe, which cannot be said entirely, and the operator which sets it down, indicated by a bar of negation, can just as well be called the not-all: $\overline{\forall}$x. ϕx.

Of this twisting and turning of the All – masked by the usage of the French signifier 'tout' (all), which applies equally to the all of the universe and to the other all – the exercise is itself limitless. Every structure in which the inscription of an All is concerned is subject to it, including the universal by means of which the twisting and turning is set forth.[1] We know that Lacan defines its modes of inscription for the sexes. To bring this about, it suffices for ϕx to be understood as the phallic function – everything then follows: man, woman, castration and the fact that there are two sexes. For the writings of the All hold also for each speaking being taken distributively, and from the fact that they are constructed as an All with respect to a ϕx, one can conclude that *each one* among them must be inscribed as subject either on one side or on the other.

But let us consider language, and put forward the following propositions: nothing exists except insofar as it is nameable in its being, and nothing is nameable except through an articulation of *lalangue*. The second proposition can always be given some meaning which will make it undeniable for anyone; as for the first, it is nothing more than an axiom whose refutation is nevertheless impossible, for if some element existed which might constitute an objection to it, it would be impossible to name it. A game of logic, no doubt, but from which a consequence follows – if in fact there exists no nameable limit to *lalangue*, it cannot be inscribed in any way on the side of the All. The collection of the elements out of which it is composed will not take on the form of the universe, nor will the claims made about it be universalisable. By contrast, both language with a small *l* and Language with a capital *L* appear as inscriptions of the All, susceptible of delineation as sites in *lalangue* of the universal. Whence it follows, reciprocally, that every universalising proposition bearing on *lalangue* is only produced out of *langue* or *langage*; whence it follows also that *langue* and *langage* cannot be sustained except by a point $\exists x. \overline{\phi x}$ which guarantees them as All.

This point has various names, but it can always be located. In the case of grammar, it is by the differences of category, by the stratification of the element within the group which includes it, by the division finally between sound and sense, that it places language on a grid and plunges it into the space of the alls; each category, each strata, limits the other, the sound suspends the sense and vice-versa. This *no* constantly referred back from one point to another is what Saussure called 'difference'. In language as Saussure defines it, just as (although less openly) in every grammar, each element is the limit and point of suspension for the other. Language, in which, as we know, there are only differences, is thus made up only of wholes, of alls. To which is added the all that it is itself for itself – Saussure constructs it by means of a *dualism*. Language being a set of signs, in other words ϕx being henceforth understood as a sign, the thing is that which, not being the sign, makes possible the simultaneous writing of $\exists x. \overline{\phi x}$ and $\forall x. \phi x$. Today, linguists, having by and large abandoned any recourse to the sign, are content to posit an extra-linguistic, whose nature and name are of little importance, since it is a matter of a pure limit, to which perhaps no reality corresponds and for which one must limit oneself to the demand that it be completely constructible.

Moreover, the division between sound and sense, stratification and dualism, these functions which guarantee the All by the suspension they assure, are themselves inscribable in the sphere of universality – in language, in fact, there are categories which suspend it. For it is easy to show[2] that certain singular elements – let us take, as brief examples, the personal pronouns – deny at once stratification (the definition in mention of the pronoun requires its use), the division into sound and sense (the meaning of *I* is the utterance of the signifier '*I*') and dualism (the thing designated by *I* consists only in a particular usage of the word which is itself a word). In order for the functions denied to be in this way by the same stroke guaranteed as All, one must no doubt allow the singular elements to be inscribed in the position of *limit* – this is the role of the concept of *shifter*. That in the operation something of the real is lost can hardly be doubted, but such is the price demanded by the All.

Logicians must obviously proceed by other routes; no doubt, they give themselves over to saving the All of each logical Language, but unlike linguists, they do not have at their disposal a universe of realities in which to delve to their heart's content for a $\exists x.\overline{\phi x}$; the required limit can come for them only from the structure of logical Languages themselves. This is what the concept of a metalanguage lends itself to, which is nothing more than the fact that whatever might be the interpretation or the power of a logical Language, there exists at least one entity which escapes it, which is this Language itself.[3] To force this point of suspension, to want Language to take itself for its object is thus necessarily to reinscribe it on the side of the not-all, whose palpable form is the paradox. It becomes apparent by contrast that the Lacanian proposition, 'there is no metalanguage', is immediately translatable as 'there is something in language which is inscribed as the not-all', and consists in nothing other than an affirmation of the existence in Language of *lalangue*.

From the perspective of *lalangue*, these operations equally productive of the All are nonetheless non-equivalent. For it is out of *lalangue* itself, once its existence is attested to, that logicians – the subtlest make no secret of it – construct the limit totalising logical Languages; all that is needed is for a name to be found for it – Tarski's everyday language, Curry's language U[4] – which puts it in its place. But linguists cannot be satisfied with this, for it is over everyday language itself that they must consolidate their hold. Far from this latter being able to function as limit, it must itself, in its own unfolding, present an inner limit, one from within. It is this which permits, to all appearances, the division between the correct and the incorrect.

But here there is an additional twist, for this partitioning sets up no limit. The *no* that it articulates is not a point of suspension, but a prohibition. Whence it follows that language, inscribed as an All, is realised in a network of obligations and interdictions. The impossible in language, which establishes it as a real, is written in the symbolism of prohibition. This is the enigma, for who will deny that the interdicted construction does not also come from language? If it were not so, it would simply be that limit where language is suspended and confirmed as the All. No need, then, for a rule stipulating that it is excluded; rightly conceived, the function of language should here suffice. Yet an explicit judgement *is* always required, for otherwise nothing in the incorrect construction would announce it as such. It is by being in certain respects *in* language that the incorrect construction demands to be dismissed from it. Yet care is needed here; such is indeed the structure of every prohibition, and the prohibition of language does not differ from this point of view from that which weighs upon the sexual.

But this cannot be grasped except in underscoring the influence of the writings of the All on the sexual. Let us assume of a speaking being that it is inscribed as subject in one of the two writing systems.[5] Provided that ϕx is understood as the phallic function, the real of its desire insofar as it is sexual is found articulated for this being in the order of the symbolic. But it is no less true to say that, from this, the family of the speaking being's imaginary identifications is generated, and in particular the system of sexed naming – 'man', 'woman' – in which is to be found captured, in reality, the real which marks speaking beings – a continuous failure to be conjoined. Thus the absolute Heteros which imposes itself in the real is written in the disparity of the writings of the All, and is imaged in the apportionment by halves of the representations issuing from the bodies: being inscribed as subject on one side or the other of ϕx, the speaking being will apprehend itself as ego, as *I*, either in the man half or the woman half.

No doubt, that to such and such a branch of writings such and such a name for the half is paired will be readily seen as contingent; but this matters little here. For us in the West, the imaginary refractions of the All and the not-all can be summed up in the respective names of man and woman. At the very most, we have learned, in modern times, that nothing in the body compels the speaking being to be inscribed, either as subject or as ego, as *I*, on one divide or other of the disparities – All or not-all, man or woman.

Let us assume for the moment of a speaking being that it is inscribed as an All – on the other hand, this being does not for an instant cease to know that some speaking beings are inscribed as the not-all. However, as for this being itself, it cannot apprehend them save from the All, which determines its position and its space. Whence it results that speaking beings, insofar as they are all, never cease to meet certain among them that they attribute to the same All and who, nevertheless, attest for it to the inscription of the not-all. Yet, this inscription is presented to them in the guise of a prohibition – for if the limit cannot be constructed, the All can no longer be said, and this impossible is converted for every speaking being into a commandment: 'Thou shalt not say all'. Through the knot of mention and use enters with these words a prohibition–the very one by which Reason ever since Kant has been guaranteed: 'Thou shalt not speak of the All'. At the same time, the negation which, in Lacanian writing, affects the operator $\forall$, allows itself with good reason to be deciphered as the μη of prohibition by which Aristotle prohibited negation from applying to the universal. To posit that the All may not be constructible has the following then as its synonym: with respect to the not-all, there is a prohibition.

Now what holds for writings holds also for their supports. Consequently, for the supports of the All, the supports of the not-all will appear also in the guise of a prohibition. Thus, for each speaking being who is inscribed as the All – which Lacanian doctrine specifies as the man's position – the not-all will be attested to in the proposition: 'there is some speaking being who is prohibited'. The support of this proposition will be a speaking being inscribed as not-all, say some woman – in general specified as the mother. The domain of the prohibition will be that in which the two inscriptions confront one another – the relation of the sexes insofar as is the case that it gives rise to writing. From which follows Oedipus – for the man, one woman – his mother – is forbidden with respect to the sexual relation.

A woman is forbidden, not insofar as she would mark the limit point of the human species (Jocasta is not the sphinx), but on the contrary insofar as she belongs to it; and by belonging to it, she supports what there is of the impossible to say about the All of the speaking being. Herein is knotted the paradox whereby what is impossible for the speaking being – the sexual relation, say – must, in addition, give rise to a prohibition.[6] It is in an exactly comparable way that what is involved in language is articulated: as All, it never ceases to come up against the possibility that it is made to deny, the not-all of *lalangue*, which comes down basically to the fact that of the extralinguistic by which the All of language must be guaranteed, nothing remains except the names which are uttered for it. The impossibility which exists of saying everything about *lalangue* in language will be distributed over the All in the guise of something prohibited, which is statable also by the following: 'some construction of *lalangue* is prohibited'. The domain of this prohibition will be that in which language and *lalangue* confront one another: the utterance. Whence a proposition – one which is only a linguistic Oedipus: 'from the point of view of language, there is some construction which is prohibited, insofar as it could be uttered'.

Once more, it is not a question of a limit point. The forbidden construction contains nothing which suspends the features of language, to the point that even a few subterfuges from time to time suffice to include it within language.[7] Despite the derisory quality of its makeup, it attests distributively in language, delineated as locus of the universal, to the not-all, namely *lalangue*, which, insofar as nothing exists to set a limit to it, cannot all be said. One thus sees why the assertion of the real of language is a homonym of the axiom by which Lacan proposes that the saying is of the order of the not-all – 'all cannot be said'. The borderline of the real that linguistics is bent on representing as the partitioning between the correct and the incorrect is made of no other substance than *lalangue* itself; it supports in its form as borderline the unlimited which undoes all universality. It is nevertheless upon this that by an astonishing effort linguistics must build in order to credit once more to the account of the universal the very thing which attests to that which is impossible to say.

Notes

1. The twistings and turnings of the All are very much in evidence in those names which tradition hands down: the World, the Universe and God. As far as the World is concerned, we know that it is unambiguously inscribed on the side of the All, since God – if only as creator – is precisely the limit which suspends it. However, should the Universe be substituted for the World, everything becomes increasingly knotted, for it is not logically excluded that God would be included within the Universe. From its now being infinite, there is nothing to prevent this from happening. Just as the Universe splits off from the world, God thus comes to be divided up.

   It would be easy to demonstrate that the God of the philosophers and scientists is this x which sets a limit to the Universe, and by this fact constitutes it as an All, within the scope of Universalising propositions. Whether this x is a reality or not is of little importance, so long as its existence is constructible; consequently, deism and atheism can be taken as equivalent to one another (and it can be seen parenthetically that Freud's atheism is necessarily linked to what Lacan calls his *touthommie* or 'allmanhood'. In return, it suffices that, through an Almighty Power, no x may be constructed which escapes the ϕx or that, through the Incarnation, God should be made Himself a value of the function. In that case, the All is no longer constructible. The support of this not-all is the God of Abraham, of Isaac and of Jacob, and just as equally the Mystery of Jesus – an all-powerful God, because He is capable of miracles, incarnate and hidden as well, insofar as He cannot be wholly said. Pascal should be read on this subject, but Newton as well.

   If God is no longer in the role of limit, it is up to another signifier to save the All of the Universe – hence this pre-eminent moment which would be its origin; or again, the insertion, in the series of phenomena, of that which denies it: liberty. One recognises what animates the Kantian antinomies and the resolution of them which practical reason proposes – but no less the detours of modern cosmologies.

   Cf. F. Regnault, 'De Deux Dieux', in *Dieu est Inconscient,*(Paris: Navarin, 1985), pp. 31–47.

2. See J.-C. Milner, 'Réflexions sur l'arbitraire du signe', *Ornicar*, 5 (1975), pp. 73–85, where the argument is worked out for the personal pronouns as well as for performatives and delocutives – which in no way exhausts the list.

3. The central claim of hermeneutics – 'there is something which always escapes Language' – is of a comparable order; it consists in positing a limit – God or Meaning – which confirms Language as All. One can in this way understand how hermeneutics is from its conception in part linked to philology.

4. See J.-A. Miller, 'Théorie de lalangue', *Ornicar*, 1 (January 1975) pp. 27–9, and 'U', *Ornicar*, 5 (1975), pp. 61–72. Tarski's article is from 1933: 'The Concept of Truth in Formalized Languages', in A. Tarski and J. H.

Woodger (trans.), *Logic, Semantics, and Metamathematics* (Oxford: Clarendon Press, 1956). H. B. Curry has returned several times to his analysis of language U; the clearest presentation is perhaps to be read in *A Theory of Formal Deducibility*, Notre Dame Mathematical Lectures, 6 (1957), where we read the following: 'The point is that everything we do depends on the U-language . . . Moreover, we can significantly-make statements about the U-language within the U-language. It follows from the foregoing that there is no such thing as meta-U-language'.

The last propositions of Wittgenstein's *Tractatus* are, negatively, equivalent: 'what we cannot speak about we must pass over in silence' evidently states a limit which retroactively constitutes the *Tractatus* as All, homologous to the All of the World introduced in the text's first proposition; but in turn, the fact that an impossible should give rise to an explicit prohibition proves that there exists at least one place where one can speak about what cannot be spoken about – this place is *lalangue*.

5. On this subject, cf. Lacan's *L'Etourdit* and lesson VII of his *Encore*.

6. That for the speaking being what is impossible should also be forbidden is then a structure which never ceases to hold when the laws of speech are at stake. Critical philosophy legislates against seeking to know the Thing in itself, because to know it is precisely impossible. There are things which it is impossible to speak of, says Wittgenstein; by this very fact, it is also forbidden to do so. If we follow Leo Strauss, Maimonides maintains at one and the same time that the disclosure of the secrets of the Torah is by nature impossible and that it is forbidden by the law (L. Strauss, *Persecution and the Art of Writing*, New York: The Free Press, 1952, p. 59). Abelard forbids himself Heloise all the more severely because he is castrated–a matter of vows and of logic.

7. The most usual type is quotation; if the sentence *P* is incorrect, it is always permissible to write the sentence *P'*: 'it is incorrect to say that P'. There are other less crude procedures. Cf. Chomsky, *Aspects*, p. 157.

6

A Desiring Linguist

What is essential to linguistics may or may not be introduced under the form of the sign. This is not to say that the choice would be inconsequential, at least when it is thought out. Quite the contrary, a lot rests on the fact that in Saussure the sign is made the support of so much that is essential, and not only in the *Course*, but everywhere else: in the studies of myth, in the analysis of anagrams, and so on. To the point that one begins to suspect it involves a more considerable investment – not only the foundations of a science, but the circumscription of a mode of being, until then unprecedented.

For one must not be afraid of exaggerating the stakes: the Saussurean texts attest to the absolutely desperate character of the aporias in which the sign is inscribed. It all comes down to a single question: from whence derives the fact that there exists the discernible? Which is equivalent to the following: how does it happen that one may think of repetition and non-repetition?

Saussure could not have been ignorant of the common answer: in order to discern, one has only to name; but this only underscored the aporia, when it was for him precisely a question of introducing discernment into that by means of which one names – let us say, to put it simply, into Language. Whence the celebrated queries – variations on Jeannot's knife[1] – what is the identity of a chess piece, of a train, when all their material elements can be modified? Or, to take up a less well known text:

> 'the rune Y is a symbol.
> 'Its IDENTITY (. . .) consists in this: that it has the form Y; that it is read Z; that it is the letter numbered eighth in the alphabet, that it is mystically called *zann*, at least when it is cited as the first in the word.

'After a short interval: . . . *it* is 10th in the alphabet . . . but already here IT begins to assume a unity (. . .).

'Where is its identity now?'[2]

In other words, each of the predicates analysing the substance can change independently of the others, in such a manner that the identity, if one wishes to circumscribe it, will have to be found elsewhere – not in the substance, but in the form; that is to say, as we have seen, in the system of differences. It is here that the concept of the sign intervenes in a crucial manner; unlike the sign of the philosophers, the Saussurean sign does not represent – it represents *for* the other signs. But unlike Lacan's signifier, no one has ever been able to say what it represented. In fact, it represents only itself – that is to say, a pure intersection, a nothing, of which one cannot even say that it is one.

For this is the paradox: the very element which should ensure discernment is crisscrossed by the multiplicity of oppositions in which it is caught; it lacks the wherewithal to insure the agency of the One. For the sign accommodates itself to a silence – it is constructed so as to foreclose the subject, whose insistence and repeated lapses circumscribe the One of each of the signifiers as it relates to another, and confer on all of them the One-by-One which structures them like a chain. Among the properties of the sign, the differential ensures the desired suture – identity is sustained only by the absence of any Self for the sign.

Thenceforth is constructed, as if *a priori*, the figure of a return of the foreclosed – for Saussure, this could only be accomplished by the reappearance of a Self out of the units of language, and which would be referable to a subject of desire. It suffices to point to the work on anagrams.

The available texts[3] have been gathered together by J. Starobinski, to whom I refer the reader here for all relevant points. They have been widely commented upon, and certain of them have already been invoked as the basis of a practical poetics. Nonetheless their implications have never been precisely determined. For this reason I will concentrate briefly on reestablishing the issues at stake.

It all begins, it seems, with a philological problem: in what does the Saturnian verse consist?

Saussure, applying the classic method for the examination of texts, discovers a first principle, that can be called the principle of the pair:

[I]n a Saturnian verse, the phonemes of each type are always paired.

With this principle, hence, only the number of phonemes is constrained, but not their nature. A more careful examination reveals that a principle governing the *choice* of the paired phonemes must be added to it; this is the principle of the anagram.

In a Saturnian verse, the phonemes are chosen on the basis of a noun, which is linked in a crucial way to the narrative meaning of the verse.

As these principles, once established, cannot be ascribed to the aleatory, and as furthermore they are non-necessary, they must be assumed to have a specific cause – a *knowledge*, explicit and conscious, of which the absence of any trace must be attributed to a *secret*.

Thus formulated, the hypothesis is in no way improbable from the point of view of the philological method. All that can be said is that it is undemonstrated; the demonstration would have to take the following form: establishing (1) that there are texts without anagrams; (2) that all confirmed anagrams are the result of a specific technique. Yet, this is what Saussure failed to do. Once defined, anagrams appeared, undeniably, everywhere – besides in Saturnian verse, in every type of Latin verse, no matter its period, even including modern verse, whose authors, consulted on the subject, neglected to answer. From that moment on, Saussure found himself in the presence of an unavoidable real, but one which philology could not deal with. There were no longer any non-necessary principles, but a property always discoverable in texts – no longer the obliterated knowledge of specialists who had themselves vanished, but the unconscious knowledge of language itself.

Nothing in all of this has any longer to do with foreclosure, and actually, it is more difficult than it would seem to establish what really rides on the anagrams.

The first thing to observe is that properly speaking the anagram denies the Saussurian sign.

– The anagram is not differential – each anagram is based on a certain noun, whose phonemes it redistributes. But it is clear that this noun (proper or common), even though it is a linguistic unit, is not treated together with what is differential. It has an identity proper to it, a Self, which it does not draw from the system of oppositions in which it would be apprehended by linguistics.

– The anagram is neither contingent nor arbitrary; its function consists in imposing a necessity on the phonemes of the verse, shielding them from the chance which marks the lexical units.
– The noun-in-anagram functions as a 'sense' and not as a signified; it is as a thing in the world – and not as the element of a language – that it is the global designation of the whole. In this sense, the anagram contravenes dualism – the order of signs and that of things are merged, and the second functions as a cause with respect to the first.
– More generally still, the anagram undermines the very principle of all linguistic or grammatical descriptions – whatever may be their methods, these assume the law of excluded middle; two units are either totally distinct, or totally collapsed; one unit is either present in a sequence, or absent. Now, let us consider the sequence *Cicuresque*, anagram of *Circe* (an example of Saussure's in Starobinski, p. 150; English translation, p. 119) or *despotique*, anagram of *désespoir* (an example of Jakobson's): to ask if the paired forms are distinct one from the other simply has no longer any meaning, since the anagram is supposed *really* still to exist in its explicit form; likewise, *Circe* or *désespoir* cannot be said to be univocally present or absent. The anagram as such determines an area where such questions, essential nonetheless to a description, are no longer relevant.

The place in the verse where the phonemes of the crucial noun are found concentrated Saussure calls the *locus princeps* (Starobinski, p. 50; English translation, p. 33): the sovereign place. Its essential attribute is that it weaves into the phonemes of the line a discrepancy which governs them. It is insofar as it differs from the elements of the explicit text that the anagrammaticised noun can be its principle of organisation. In other words: (1) insofar as it embodies a difference and (2) insofar as it is *one*. To which the *locus princeps* adds that this principle is included in the verse as one of its parts.

One could easily maintain that the anagrammaticised noun is nothing other than the verse itself, considered as a succession of phonemes, concentrated in a single point: the One of the noun embodying the One which governs the verse, insofar as *one* verse and as divisible into discernible elements, *one* by *one*. In this sense, the *locus princeps*, or sovereign place, is an appropriate enough image of the master signifier – the signifier One of the 'there exists some One in the signifying chain', included in the signifying chain.

The distance from the *Course* could thus not be greater. There, everything was governed by differentiation, so that it was impossible to establish any imaginary representative whatsoever, grouping within itself the set of the intervals and differences governing language; here, by contrast, differentiality is undone and what remains of it takes the entirely positive figure of a sovereign place, of a place by rights locatable in every verse.

In the second place, it should be said outright that the anagrams are in no way illusory. On the contrary, they touch upon a real: that of homophony. Everything rests, in Saussure's arguments, on the fact that one sequence of phonemes can always echo another, and through this signify it cryptogrammatically. Now, the fact that this is necessarily the case goes without saying, requiring only a little careful attention. Open randomly any text whatsoever – Meillet tried the experiment – and anagrams abound, impossible to stamp out.

Only, with this real of homophony, condition for the slip of the tongue and the pun, linguistics has nothing to do. It sets it aside, ascribing it to the contingent. This the Saussurian sign easily accommodates: if it is contingent that a particular phonic signifier is attached to a particular signified, *a fortiori* the same will hold if two phonic signifiers attached to different signifieds should happen to be grouped together. These are accidents in the order of things, which cannot affect the order of signs.

This is not to say that linguistics always forgoes treating the real of homophony, but it will do so in reducing it to its core of contingence and in subjecting it to the excluded middle of distinctiveness. Comparative grammar is thus entirely based on the observation that, in a given language and especially from language to language, there are echoes, but it is well known that their cause is statable as a linguistic set whose status is regular – for example, Indo-European – governed in this case by the usual principles. In the same way, and by a natural extension Saussure, confronted with another homophony, attempts to integrate it into the field of philology, in ascribing it to an entirely contingent cause: a noun, an ordinary lexical unit, chosen by a technician for the purpose of coding, and continuing to exist, distinct, as a cryptographic key.

The anagram is thereby revealed to be ambiguous. On the one

hand, it bespeaks the fact that homophony belongs to language, as the object of linguistics; but on the other hand, it bespeaks the fact that it is not assimilable to language. For this reason, the anagram can restore the required contingence only in denying the standard properties of the sign. It represents, in a philological system of language, what in it marks its dependence with respect to a real against which it cannot be measured.

The anagram thus represents, within the system of the impossible of language an 'in addition' which is distinguished from it. On the one hand, it is entirely formulable in terms of phonemes and presupposes an analysis based, in this case, on the principle which makes homophony contingent – so that the latter acquires its status only through a system which devalues it. On the other hand, it denominates a real which exceeds every possible phonology. In this way, through the intractability of its real it places language in excess, whether considered in itself or in its calculable representation. This function of excess we will call *lalangue*.

Nevertheless, the essential is perhaps not yet reached, for the ambiguity of the anagram very readily lends itself to any human science whatsoever, and through it the real of homophony can give rise, just like anything else, to deduction and notation. This is, moreover, what one observes since, thanks to Jakobson, what was a failure from the point of view of philology, is turned into a success measurable from the point of view of structural linguistics through the intermediary of poetics. By the same token, language as a system of the impossible regains its territory and extends its frontiers. What might seem to exceed it is no longer attributable to an effect of the real, but to an imaginary figure: poetic genius. As often happens, what cannot be assimilated to calculable representations is credited to humanist culture. The Saussurian anagram becomes the modern figure of the trope, means of commentary, through a compromise which reconciles to one another poetry and the science of language.

But it should be clear that Saussure had something quite different in mind. Unlike Jakobson, poetry scarcely interested him and he would not have been satisfied to come up with a plausible way of talking about it; as he understood it, he was dealing with truth, in the guise which alone counted for him – speculation on Indo-European. And it was of little importance to him if, via this speculation, he found yet another approach to the cultural forms of the humanist tradition. What he was searching for was a knowledge.

The anagrams must spell out the initiatory knowledge, secret and forgotten, of the Indo-European poets, and if it is impossible to treat them as such, better to ignore them, because in this case they are without value – so, lacking the conclusive evidence, Saussure would grow silent on the subject. It is because of this that he became a scandal, as much for the sympathisers, Jakobson or Starobinski (a knowledge? by no means), as for the orthodox scholars, the latter perhaps coming closer to the heart of the matter when they speak of madness. For this is indeed what is rumoured, and no doubt explains the embargo placed on the manuscripts in Geneva.

What makes the knowledge in this case so shocking? The reason is simple: it is impossible to come to terms with the real of the anagrams, completely intertwined with language, in acting as if linguistics did not exist. And as we know, linguistics wants to know nothing of what it is that underlies the anagrams. But what this implies is not that it wants to remain ignorant; but rather it wishes for no knowledge to be statable in this area. Which one can of course comply with in two ways: one consists in acting as if there was nothing to remark – this is the current practice. The other is to confine oneself to the love of the poets. But Saussure holds out; he is bent on articulating a knowledge and, being able to conceive of it only under a single form, exhausts himself by supposing a subject for this knowledge.

Such is no doubt the locus of the madness, in which Saussure overtakes what one could imagine to be Cantor's madness: that, from the heart of science, a subject should recognise, in the real that he finds, the lineaments of a knowledge and that he devote himself to subjectivising it. This subject supposed for the knowledge of sets Cantor named God,[5] making mathematics the servant of theology; Saussure named it *vates*, making linguistics the servant of legend.[6]

What is fundamental then is that Saussure should have posited in terms of a subjectivisable knowledge the point where *lalangue* is tied to language. An imaginary knowledge no doubt, since it scarcely does anything but fill in the untraversable space separating one from the other – but at least Saussure did not give in to making the latter bearable through recourse to the cultural. On the contrary, by not letting go of it, he had a brush with madness – in this regard the descriptions should be reread (Starobinski, pp. 38–40; English translation, pp. 26–8) in which Saussure conjures up the scene of the *vates* counting with the aid of sticks the relevant phonemes, thereby carrying out exactly what the philologist turns out retroactively to have to repeat. Saussure thus becomes in fact the point of subjectivity that he supposed in this knowledge, and the research on the anagrams turns into the exhausting and vain reenactment of a primal scene, in which, in the unfolding of a story and the subjectivisation of the *locus princeps*, the distance from language to what exceeds it is bridged.

As for what gives substance to the function of excess, that it should be homophony and not something else, is a direct result of the concept of the sign. By means of it, language is thought of as calculable in what it possesses of differentiality. The foreclosed could thus return only under the form of that which undoes differentiality: the contingent echo.

In this respect, Chomsky constitutes what amounts to a counter-demonstration. For him, unlike Saussure, the discernible in language causes no problems and requires no notion peculiar to it. It is simply given and observed.[7] From this point on, the differential and the sign play no distinctive role in the establishment of a grammatical notation. By way of consequence, homophony can no longer exert a deconstructive effect. It is simply out of the picture, the existence or non-existence of anagrams or of poetry having no relevance for the form of grammatical theory. This is not to say, however, that the foreclosed subject will not return, but only that it will not spring up in the same places.

As could have been expected, to the very extent that the integration of linguistics into the domain of the sciences is with Chomsky more completely attained, this returned operates, as with all scientists, under the form of an ethic of equality and liberty. Thus he who has reduced speaking beings to the status of a calculable point dedicates himself to making their condition bearable for them, in militating for their political liberation. But here, it can be seen, nothing any longer distinguishes the linguist from any other subject of science. Saussure's singularity fades as the extraction of language from *lalangue* can be considered more completely accomplished.

Notes

1. Martha Robert's introduction to her French translation of Lichtenberg's aphorisms begins: 'The name of Lichtenberg scarcely invokes anything more for the French reader than the famous "Knife without a blade whose handle is missing", even though the paternity of this unusual object may not invariably be attributed to him without hesitation'. 'Introduction' to Georg Christophe Lichtenberg, *Aphorisms*, Preface by André Breton, Martha Robert (trans.), (Paris:Jean-Jacques Pauvert, 1966) p. 21. [Translator's note.]
2. Saussure, in J. Starobinski, *Les Mots sous les mots* (Paris: Gallimard, 1971) pp. 15–16; *Words Upon Words: The Anagrams of Ferdinand de Saussure*, Olivia Emmet (trans.) (New Haven: Yale University Press, 1979) p. 5.
3. It should be recalled that only a few texts were published. Those which survived were subsequently not allowed to see the light of day by those in Geneva responsible for Saussure's papers.
4. Roman Jakobson, 'Une Microscopie du Dernier "Spleen" dans *Les Fleurs du Mal*',*Questions de Poétique* (Paris: Seuil, 1973), p. 435.
5. Cf. G. Cantor, *Abhandlungen Mathematischen u. Philosophischen Inhalts*, (letter to Cardinal Franzelin of 22 January 1886, pp.399–400, and the letter to professor Eulenburg of 28 February 1886, pp. 400–7).
6. See Starobinski, *Les Mots* p. 36; English translation, pp. 22–3, as well as the equation on p. 38; English translation, p. 24: 'to satisfy either the god, or poetic law'.
7. I indicate in passing that the givenness of the discernible comes down to constituting the speaking subject as a text to be deciphered. Through the concept of *competence*, it is stated that grammatical theory is already written in subjects by the mere fact that they can speak the language (cf. *Aspects*, p. 25). It is thus not immaterial that some of the most prominent representatives of transformational grammar are Jewish by origin, trained in Talmudic exegesis.

7

On Language

To be is to be nameable. Now there is no name that is not speakable – but does this not presuppose that a being has spoken? This is to say that from the being to the speaking the circle is without end. A being does not come to be qualified as speaking without a certain uneasiness: it cannot be that the being is here a bare substratum, to which the property 'speaking' comes to be attached, even if as an essential attribute. Rather, the speaking being is one whose being itself does not fail to be affected by the fact that it speaks – since the speakable name which raises it up to being presupposes that, somewhere at least there has been speaking.

Whether or not a single speaking being – God or otherwise – exists, this being is a *parlêtre*. The being in it and the speaking are not disconnected and corrupt one another. But finally what does this speaking being speak? What must it be to enable and to require its being to be inscribed there in suspension?

It very clearly could not be the language of linguists that is involved: a mathematisable representation cannot in any case affect the being which sustains it, and furthermore as the object of science language is precisely maintained as not being spoken by anyone whose being is specifiable. Nor could Language with a capital *L* be involved. An essential attribute of the human species, it presupposes a previous being, which it contributes to specifying as Man. Like philosophy itself, from which it derives, it repeats the disjunction of the being and its properties.

The speaking being presupposes a name, but the name presupposes the speaking being. The statement of the circle gives rise by itself alone to the semblance of its resolution: the name which calls to being the *parlêtre* – in fact, the very name *'parlêtre'* – can continue to exist only as a lack since, during the time which precedes the utterance of the name, the *parlêtre* which utters it is missing. The set of grammatical constructions in which the name *parlêtre* should occur will thus be, structurally, always failing, the operator all will never be legitimate, if applied to it. In short this set is not all. The *parlêtre* can be specified only by that which names the not-all of namings – *lalangue*.

It is in this register moreover that the Witz *'parlêtre'* itself reverberates, sufficient indication of the relation: *lalangue is that by which a being can be said to be speaking*. The two concepts are merely one and the same concept and are distinguished only by their point of view. Hereafter, every question about *lalangue* can be translated into a question about the speaking being, and is found to depend in the final analysis upon the following question: what is a speaking being?

To introduce the possibility of one, Lacan deliberately adopts a classical style. It is, he says, because two beings cannot be joined together that they speak. A thesis entirely philosophical in appearance, whose most undisguised formulation can be found in Géraud de Cordemoy's *Discours Physique de la Parole*, but the tradition goes a good deal farther back. The thesis generally takes on its meaning via the construction of the contrary hypothetical case: take that of pure spirits – angels, for example; nothing comes to raise an obstacle to their union. Knowing immediately everything about one another, they have no need for Language. By which the following is implied: (1) that the crucial relation between two beings is the knowledge, the acquaintance, they can come to have of one another; (2) that the place of this knowledge being the mind, the body constitutes the crucial obstacle.

It is easy to guess that this is not what interests Lacan. What, however, confers its value on the classical thesis is that it links the possibility of Language to the existence of a particular impossible, marking a particular relation. For the philosopher, the terms of the relation are subjects of representation, endowed with a mind and a body, the second representing the first; the relation is one of knowledge via the intermediary of a representation, otherwise known as a communication;[1] the impossible is sustained by the body. Of this account nothing remains in Lacan except the model – the terms are desiring subjects, the relation is the sexual relation, what sustains it are the bodies, not insofar as they represent the movement of the mind, but insofar as they are cut up, fretted by desire. In the same way, then, as the Language of philosophy is the site of the impossible of mutual knowledge, so likewise *lalangue* is the site of the impossible of the sexual relation.

One can see from whence the communication model draws its force when it comes to representing Language; it is that it is cut exactly to the dimensions of the real of which Language is the phantasy. The pair of interlocuters that the model unites is the faithful image, and thereby the most appropriate mask, of the impossible conjoining of two desiring subjects. Now, we have seen, all linguistics is based on a communication model (or its equivalent).[2] In this sense, it takes its internal coherence from the phantasmatic: the representation of the act of Language with a capital *L*, supposedly the condition for language with a small *l*, is turned into a grimacing mimicry of the real in which *lalangue* is established.

Two subjects which cannot be joined together – such is the knot of *lalangue*. In other words, two speaking beings are necessarily and really distinct, and from no point of view can their difference be overcome – not even conceptually. They never cease to be written as discernible, and no real can exist where they are made symmetrical. It is in this way that the communication model – that of Saussure, for example – functioning as a representation, functions also as a mask. Its essential property consists in effect in applying to the impossible relation of conjunction the principle of symmetry and of indiscernibles, two speaking subjects in the sense of linguistics being by definition considered only under the features which make them equivalent one to the other. In this way, the non-conjunction is maintained in the framework, but in such a way that it is always possible to deny it and to compensate for it by the equality and symmetry of the terms. In truth, Language, as a concept, and language, as the underpinning of a real, are nothing other than this compensation itself. They fill in the chasm of non-conjunction, magically converting its effects into so many indications to the contrary. The topology of non-conjunction becomes the space of communication; the heterogeneous collection of the *parlêtres* is counted as the homogeneous one of partners in an exchange, the snatches of grammatical constructions are made into a message.

What is thus revealed is a singular relation of language to love. For love must also compensate for an impossible conjunction: the very one captured by Lacan in the formula, 'there is no sexual relation'. Moreover, one should try the following experiment: take any schema of communication whatsoever and introduce into it, instead of speaking subjects, entirely calculable, subjects barred by desire, and one obtains the form of a love. The difference, of course, erupts in the manner of the desire's insistence, but this counts perhaps less than the homology – in love as in language, it is a matter of eliminating the discernible, of making it so that it ceases to be written, so that the two become one, by a phantasmatic bridging of the unconjoinable. In addition, the operation borrows the same means, those of the sign. Cordemoy said it well enough: the language-dependent relation is erected upon the fact that a speaking subject surmises that the being it is face to face with is not only a like being, but a self-same one, that is to say, a speaking subject the same as it; it need only in this case recognise in certain physical movements signs and as a consequence assume for them a transmitting subject. It is in the same fashion, Lacan says, that for a gesture, for a word, in short for a spoken sentence, a desiring subject presupposes another subject, that it would love insofar as one was the same as the other with respect to desire.

Why should it be surprising then if from love to language one moves by making them reversible, as all the varieties of *préciosité* attest, if one joins them one to the other, to the point that the love of language and the lies of love, far from counting as alliances of words, attest to the oneness of a common concern: the 'self-sameness' compensating for the impossible conjunction? Both are rooted then in *lalangue*, insofar as it is the site of this impossibility.

There is one difference, however: wherever love is interlaced with desire and denies the necessity of *lalangue*, it is out of desire that language acts as if love did not exist, and it is out of *lalangue* that it constructs its material. Consequently, it is from language alone that one can hope for access to *lalangue*; but the homology of love can be of help here. The fact that *lalangue* exists in effect comes down to saying, as we have seen, that love is possible, that the sign of a subject can cause desire, that a subject of desire can give a sign in a chain: it is in this way that *lalangue* exceeds language and imprints on it the mark by which it can be recognised.

Given a sequence of language, it is enough for a subject of desire to give a sign in it at one point, for everything by one and the same stroke to founder – the calculability of syntax ceases, grammatical representation caves in and the articulated elements turn into signifiers. This process, which, following J. A. Miller, taking up a term of Lacan's, I will call subjectivisation, can operate anywhere; all that it requires is a chain and a point that is distinguished within it. The subject, in this sense, has the freedom of indifference and all places can be occupied by its desire.

Let us assume that language, as the system of the impossible and as the object of a knowledge, is subject to this process – at once the function of excess – which is *lalangue* – takes shape within it. This is the set of all possible chains – those that science represents: etymology, various paradigms, derivations, transformations, and so on, and those that it refuses to recognise: homophonies, homosemies, palindromes, anagrams, tropes, and all imaginable figures of association. *Lalangue* is thus a throng of proliferating arborescences, to which the subject fastens its desire, any node or knot capable of being selected by it in order there to give a sign. The point of subjectivisation is always one among many, and the chain in which it is distinguished is no sooner delineated than a thousand analogous chains spring up: swarming, as Lacan says. Any chain of any language whatever, insofar as a subject can give a sign in it – such could then be a definition of *lalangue*. But it really goes into operation only from the moment when a subject of desire has, in the chain, subjectivised a point, in other words, when it has spoken its desire. In this sense. *lalangue* is equally as well, in the proliferation of its associations, the virtual set of the statements of desire. To this statement, *lalangue* offers its resources, and they are borrowed for whatever they are worth – including in its unconscious dimension.

In this respect, the characteristic step of linguistics and of grammar boils down to constructing a representation of the chains of association. The fundamental notion becomes then that of the paradigm, by means of which the chains are converted into stateable and regular tables. One can understand the peculiar status that the theory of the paradigmatic occupies in Saussure – it is the critical point where language is extracted from *lalangue*, only certain associations being retained, the others being henceforward condemned to exceed the representation and to continue to exist as repressed in the form of an unconscious knowledge.

But the speaking being is not generally satisfied with this enumerative approach – it requires something which represents *lalangue* without adulterating it, an image of that which exceeds representation. The itinerary is necessarily imaginary, if only because it is reflexive – it is a matter of the speaking being going back to what makes it a speaking being and stabilizing this with an imaginable totality and permanence. Here opens up a gallery of well known figures, of which the principal is the mother tongue, which is not *lalangue* but a received image of its function of excess with respect to grammars and theories. One must add here all ideal languages – that of Brisset, but also the basic language of Schreber, and the language of Wolfson, obtained by addition from all non-maternal languages. Here it is a matter of totalities definable in extension; elsewhere, the definition is intensional – thus the surplus-purity of Mallarmé. In every case one obtains, included among the possible languages, a term which exceeds them all, as if standing in for the representation of the function of excess itself.

The function of the anagrams is easily enough seen in this way; but perhaps the analysis should be pushed further. On several occasions we have, among the chains of association, invoked etymology, and notably those which make Indo-European possible.[3] Up till now, the latter has been apprehended only as an object of science, and as the figure of a knowledge in which Saussure hoped to write the anagrams out in an integral fashion. Yet a suspicion arises, in light of the rumor which Indo-Europeanists repeat among themselves – namely, that their discipline time and again brushes up against madness. This suspicion is reinforced again when the entirely peculiar type of linguistic science to which comparative grammar aspires is recognised, as well as the type of data which engenders it.

In fact, let us take things from the beginning – phonic echoes from language to language had been observed from time immemorial, and in particular between Greek and Latin. Was this fact to be ascribed to contingence or to a general necessity of phonetic articulation, or finally, in the case of homophonies, was it necessary to infer a specific cause? The problem was able to receive a precise formulation, and as a matter of fact, which makes it a rare case, it has been entirely resolved – from 1880 on, exactly what was involved had become clear.

The homophonies considered are neither absolutely contingent nor absolutely necessary; they have a specific cause which is describable as a community of origins. This is the concept of Indo-European: as can be seen, it is analysed into two parts: (a) the phonetic resemblances have a cause; (b) this cause is a language. In other words, Indo-European is the language which causes the homophonies from language to language. To be an Indo-Europeanist then is (a) to construct a language, the language of the cause, (b) to link each form of the observed languages to a form of the language-cause (this is what is called etymology). One immediately sees the strangeness of the notion of Indo-European – it is a language in the full sense of the word, at every point comparable to every known language, but it will never be attested to as spoken by subjects. In effect, if by chance one were to describe observable traces, they could be held to be only the elements of a language-effect, the sought for language-cause still eluding the description.[4]

In short, Indo-European is not simply a dead language, like Latin, which is no longer spoken, but which it is always possible to ascribe to subjects. Indo-European is itself never in the position of being considered a mother tongue for subjects, even ones who have disappeared. At first sight, we have here a language which is entirely the elucubration of knowledge.

Is this to say that it must be treated as some sort of Esperanto, concocted for rational ends, with a view to eliminating all traces of an excess in which a subject might have given a sign? It is the contrary which is true – each Indo-European form is in itself a knot of associations, at once the origin and the echo of a set of observed forms, which are found thus grouped together in a series of indefinite crisscrossings. The etymological dictionary is presented in fact as an arborescence with endless branchings, offered for a subject to be inscribed in it. No doubt, unlike, for example, what one finds in Bloch-Wartburg, the law of the series is not supported by a single document: everything is a matter of the reconstruction of knowledge. But this knowledge itself is completely infected by a desire, that of the Indo-Europeanist for, after all, what can become attached to the reconstruction of a language of which no one will ever perceive a single element, if not a desire? Whence, moreover, the ludicrous side which, for the reasonable mind, characterises comparative grammar; every form that it produces presents this mélange of passion and futility which gives evidence of a surplus-of-thrills.

For Indo-Europeanists – but one must be one at least an instant in order to preceive it – Indo-European is the set of all the arborescenes of particular languages, the matrix and the writing of all equivocations, flattened out into the form of a language.[5] In this sense, it concentrates within itself and embodies those points that, in each particular language, would betray an agency which exceeds it. It is these very points which constitute a cause for Indo-Europeanists, and arouse their desire so far as language is concerned. This desire can be stated thus: to write the excess itself, to write *lalangue*.

In the process, a node, a knot, is described where knowledge, writing and *lalangue* as the place of equivocations intersect and blend. For Indo-European notes the arborescences in a regulated and constrained writing via phonetic laws – and in return permits the re-introduction of the discernible into each language. Still more, it is Indo-European which supposedly maintains what there is of the One in each Indo-European language. What we encounter once again then is the concept of the master-signifier, signifying what there is of the One in every signifying order, and for each signifier of this order. In this sense, Indo-European is the master-signifier incarnate for each particular language.

But here this is a general fact, true of all ideal languages, and one which touches upon the very essence of languages. After all, even if one can disclose in all grammars and all linguistics a core of misconception, this perhaps counts for less than the simple fact that grammar and linguistics are possible. Now this presupposes one thing, which is in no way trivial: languages are transcribable in such a way that everything in them is discernible from everything else, in other words they reveal that the One exists. So the question arises: where does the One in the various languages come from? From the master-signifier, it will be answered, but this implies at the same time the continuous possibility that the existence of the discernible must be ascribed to a signifier placed in the position of agent: the agent of the discernible, that is to say none other but the Master.

Here is the explanation of what we had previously observed – that the Language of mastery is literally obsessive when it comes to grounding the discernible in language; the law, the rule, the arbitrary, all these various names converge towards a unique centre: the signifier of the One, put in the position of acting upon language. No doubt, linguists and grammarians can come to terms with this in various ways. There are those who speak openly to the Master, and no one since Richelieu can ignore the intimate connection established between the regulation of language and the maintenance of order among peoples (that the comparativists had more taste for Nazism than for parliamentary democracies, that formalist linguists are generally liberal and modernist introduces only anecdotal variations). There are those who close off entirely the question of the origin of the One – as does Chomsky, only to pay for the operation of a return of the figure of the Master under the explicit form of political militancy.[6] There are finally those, rarer still, who, having recognised the question, take upon themselves the weight of its solution. They subjectivise within themselves the position of the agent of the One, making themselves the support of that which introduces the discernible into language. Such is, I believe, the key to Saussure, qua subject – the madness, in fact, does not begin in him with the anagrams; it is already in the *Course*. It is one and the same move which leads him to wish to maintain the One in the midst of the sonorous equivocations of Latin verse and in the midst of every possible language, by the differential. The *Course*, recognised by academics, and the pages of a poetics, unknown to them, repeat the same line, the one which without a doubt articulated Saussure's desire: the One which marks languages comes to them from outside.

For this is indeed what is at stake – nothing, in languages, lead one to think that they are transcribable as signifiers. This is a power which exceeds them. What other than a legislator, divine or not, individuated or not, subjectivised or not, but in any case a Master, could account for it? But this is precisely what Lacan would not accept. If the master-signifier is incarnated, it is not in an agent, it is in *lalangue,* insofar as all the forms of agents are its effects. At this point once again is found the proposition: if there is a One in languages – if then linguistics is possible – this is because *lalangue* exists, because speaking beings, as such, cannot be joined together.

Notes

1. By communication, obviously the mathematical concept should not be understood, but the concept of the philosophers: the relation of mutual knowledge between two subjects, taken in the space of representation – that is to say, endowed with a mind and a body.
2. For example, Chomsky explicitly denies any importance to the function of communication for the theory of Language. But he rediscovers its equivalent, in projecting this theory onto a unique subject; instead of

mutual knowledge, Language has for its function the disentanglement for the subject of its own representations. Here one encounters again the move by which Chomsky projects the speaker-hearer pair onto a unique speaking subject. These are only variations of style.

3. This is not the place to distinguish the various types of etymology possible. Let us simply say that Indo-European etymology has little relation to the etymology illustrated in Bloch-Wartburg, the first having to do with relative temporal ordering and structural proofs, the second with absolute datings and documentary proofs. Finally these two disciplines, within the framework of science, are to be distinguished from ancient etymology – that of Varron or of Isidore of Seville – which is properly a part of rhetoric.

4. The history of comparative grammar is on this point exemplary: by turn several real languages were able to play the role of the language-cause incarnate – thus Sanskrit, and much later, Hittite. Each time, the discipline developed in treating them each in turn as language-effects.

5. In this respect, Indo-European is not unrelated to the deep structure of the transformationalists. There are, however, two differences: (1) deep structure is defined by not being able on its own to represent a language, while the set of Indo-European forms is a language in the full sense of the word; (2) the writing of Indo-European does not belong to logic.

6. We can add here the atypical heroes – Pierre Guiraud, for instance, who, linguist in the full sense of the term, nonetheless keeps open that fissure that we all devote ourselves to filling in – should one read his *Structures étymologiques du lexique français* (Paris: Larousse, 1967) and his two *Villons, Le Gay Savoir de la Coquille*, (Paris: Gallimard, 1968) and *Le Testament de Villon* (Paris: Gallimard, 1970) one would see there the gay science of homophony at work, decked out, at the appropriate moment, with Carnival finery. As for the figure of the signifier One, it is plainly outlined there: does not Guiraud have a treatise on the sexual vocabulary? See his *Dictionnaire Erotique* (Paris: Payot, 1982).

8

On the Linguist

Up to this point, the approach we have privileged has been that starting from linguistics – which, after all, makes us scarcely distinguishable from the epistemologists. On the other hand, one question remains open, and one which can find expression only in psychoanalytic discourse: what of the linguist?

The basic proposition, in this regard, is the following: linguistics in and of itself creates no social bond; it succeeds in doing so only in and through the University. In this sense, there is no linguistic discourse, but only a special case of academic discourse. No doubt one could say the same thing today of the greater part of the disciplines laying claim to the title of 'science', but we know that the connection of science with the University is not an essential one. It has not always existed, and even today when in fact it does, it would be easy to indicate the points of rupture – the scientist qua scientist is not a professor. But the sciences called human constitute an exception – psychology, sociology, etc. and linguistics are possible only through the process which, out of every segment of discernible reality, can create the material for a knowledge. Yet this process is itself possible only through the placement of knowledge in the position of agent – in other words by the constitution of an academic discourse defined by the agent knowledge, the indefinite production of gaping subjects, and a master, the truth of this arrangement.

That, in this venture, linguistics should happen to confront a real, while the others remain at the level of the phantasmatic, is not at this point significant. Linguistics is in no way responsible for this, but only its object. There is in this a surprising twist; linguistics (to which one can add grammar) encounters the real

128

which governs it only in conferring on it certain properties which make it representable: permanence, univocalness, regularity, just so many tokens for the simple fact that a real returns always to its place. Now, these properties are found to be also what renders language not only teachable, but also the vehicle of whatever teaching is possible.

For the University and, even where its discourse has not had a visible presence, every form of School, both presuppose not only speaking beings and *lalangue,* but also that the latter homogenises these beings permanently, hence that it is thus made subject to the principle of the same and the repeatable, or hence that it is interpretable as one language. One here reaches the substratum shared by the core of a real and a phantasmatic institution. To say that there is no grammar save through and for language is to say in the same breath that there is no grammar save for the School, that there is no School save through grammar.[1] In this configuration, linguistics alters nothing, save only in presupposing the conjunction of science and teaching. Unlike grammar, then, it has an identifiable birth, the comparative grammar of the classical languages hardly capable of appearing elsewhere than in the German University where the crucial conjunction occurred.

There is one ancillary but ever verifiable consequence: from the knowledge of language, whether or not it is inscribed within science, one can expect no other use than that of making pedagogy more rational. However disinterested this or that researcher might here wish to be, the School will hound them all and demand a reckoning from them.

The correlate of a knowledge of language can therefore only be the subject produced by the configuration in which the knowledge is agent. Linguists, by definition, study and teach – hence the importance of academic recognition for them. Even the real with which they are concerned makes itself felt as such only through a continual support – the kind they ensure insofar as subjects, but which individual linguists cannot pursue without the guarantee offered by the 'likes'[2] of them, fellow-linguists, produced like them by the action of knowledge. Whence it follows that unre-cognised linguists are a contradiction in terms, for otherwise the real of their object would disintegrate before their eyes and, like an actor without a public, nothing would any longer come to confirm them in their being. There is nothing left for the linguist, as for Nietzsche, philologist unacknowledged by his peers, than to play with masks and to dance on the tight rope.

It remains nonetheless true that linguists are directly concerned with *lalangue* – comparable in this to psychoanalysts, from whom everything else divides them, and distinct from the other practitioners of the human sciences, to whom everything unites them. Therein lies the subtlety which Lacan credits their case with. In what sense it remains to be seen.

We recall the two theses which set forth the object of linguistics:

– language supports the not-all of *lalangue*.
– language is an all, a whole.

Lalangue is marked by the not-all in that it always falls short of, is wanting in, the truth. This not-all manifests itself in a series of impossible points – to think of language is to posit that these points form a system and that this system is representable. It is to think, moreover, that it is representable as an all, a whole, whereby one obtains in their contradictory conjunction the two initial propositions – language is the all of the not-all.

Henceforth, the relation of linguistics to *lalangue* is necessarily a subtle relation to the not-all. Doubtless, linguistics can grasp the real with which it is concerned only by starting from the All. But this real is realised, in and of itself, only by way of the not-all; it marks *lalangue* only inasmuch as it is, structurally, what makes it impossible for the truth to be wholly said. The defects that one cannot fail to locate in language with respect to *lalangue* serve only to displace onto the representation the continual failure of *lalangue* itself with respect to the truth.

For the set drawn from *lalangue* to be thought of as an All, a Whole, it is thus necessary for the mechanism which consigns *lalangue* to the not-all to be elided. Truth becomes the limit, authorising, by its very exclusion, universalising propositions. It is in order to bracket its agency that linguistics circumscribes its object, and if necessary, it is perfectly capable of saying so openly. Here we touch upon the ultimate effect of the dualism which we have seen supports it – if the order of words and that of things must be kept apart, it is less in order to set aside visions of the world than because things here come to stand as representatives of the site of truth.

For let us reconsider yet again the Saussurian terms; the sign ceases to be defined by its association with a thing. By 'thing' must be understood thoughts about things ('concepts') as well as material things – that is, the class of all that a sign can be associated with. What is therefore at stake are not things as such, but the relation of association itself. By the same token, the target appears – truth, insofar as it is thought of as the very concept of adequate association (of a thought to a thing, of a word to a thing, of a thought to a word). By way of dualism, Saussure, and every linguist after him, elides every agency from which a value designated precisely as one of truth could come to the sequences of language.

It is thus because truth is the class of relations of adequation, and every x which enters into such a relation with an element of language will take the figure of truth – that, of necessity, there must be nothing to which language may be said to be adequate. But the knot of this necessity is that there must be no truth for language to be grasped as an all, a whole, one which is wanting in nothing.

But once this is said, truth does not cease to exist; in consequence of which *lalangue* does not cease to exert a pressure in language and to undo its integralness. Linguistics, having for its object an all, undergoes the law of the all. It must go over it thoroughly as a whole, condemned to exhaustiveness as to its extension and to consistency as to its intension. But at the same time, it must recognise points where the not-all leaves its mark and introduces its disquieting strangeness into the chains of regularity. As a result of this fact, consistency is affected, with the result that two imperatives contradict one another. There can be no exhaustiveness without inconsistency, nor consistency without inexhaustiveness.

But the operations of *lalangue* are also always such that they can be covered over, and subterfuges are possible. Encountering a critical point, linguistics must notate it, if it wishes to be exhaustive, and in such a way as not to create inconsistency for the rest of the notation. Hence the invention of symbols with double meaning, simultaneously notating, covering over, and attesting to present instances of failure.

A few examples are in order:

– The very concept of language – on the one hand it designates an abstract totality, and one which is denumerable, condemned, as soon as it is represented, to the status of phantasy; this is language-reality, whether one interprets it as institution, as competence, as national emblem, as set of practices, or whatever. But on the other hand, and without it being possible to separate the various strands, language sustains the bar of the impossible which marks *lalangue* in its relationship with the truth, and which it is literally impossible to totalise. Here is quite obviously the primal double meaning, which all the others are in some sense tokens of.

- The categories (noun, verb, adjective, and so on) – on the one hand, they constitute the reference points for the enumeration of language, and are an integral part of its representation;[3] on the other hand, they embody the One in *lalangue*, and by their possibility alone, the operation of the master signifier is brought about in it.

- The subject of the utterance or enunciation – on a first reading, we have here a positive concept of linguistics, which, for the purpose of pure description, must distinguish it from the subject of the statement or enouncement.[4] Simply at the level of phenomena, were it only to think the possibility of the *I*, it must posit that every statement can be referred to this point, about which one presupposes nothing except that it utters. But immediately such a concept is open to another reading: the point to which the utterance is referred is at the same time posited as a subject, and the possibility remains that it subjectivises the statement in a way which escapes representation. This is what the notorious so-called expletive *ne* attests to: trace of the subject of the utterance or enunciation, not insofar as it still continues to exist as the point to which every utterance is to be referred, but on the contrary insofar as it disappears in every utterance – not a permanence without dimension, but the dimension of a disappearance.

Nevertheless, this subject to which one refers the unconscious vow of the expletive *ne*, and the one which weights utterances with its permanence and calibrates the denumerable set of shifters, is indeed the same existence. It is simply open to a double meaning – linguistics is always permitted, in order to satisfy the demands of exhaustiveness, to assign it to a category – for example, that of the shifters; but in so doing it introduces into its notation something heterogeneous, which will eventually make it prey to inconsistency; to observing, for example, that the subject of the utterance may disappear anywhere in the sequences and infect them with its indefinable vacillation.

Similar examples abound – some can be found in the theory of tenses and moods, in the grammar of insults, that of questions and their responses in dialogue. But in the final analysis they all come down to the same thing. From whence it follows that, since linguistics is completely shot through with the *double entendre*, each subject says something about itself in choosing one reading of it. By virtue of this at least linguistics merits being taken as a guide, since to each subject it returns the detour each preferred, the thesis about the speaking being that it wanted to hear.

But this is true of linguists themselves; it is incumbent on them to choose their own understanding of the symbols they manipulate, and should the occasion arise, to choose not to be ignorant of *lalangue* from which their object is extracted, nor of the not-all which constantly marks its totalities. Doubtless – and this is the general case – a few spiritual additives will suffice here – a linguist during the week, one reads poetry on the Sabbath. But from time to time there are those who are not content with this. At every point of their construction they pick out instances of the not-all, returning, like the ghost of the king, to haunt the order that his disappearance has allowed to be reproduced.

This can mean only one thing: to language is restored the dimension of truth which renders it wanting, no longer under the form of a value measuring an adequation, but insofar as it attests to the articulation of desire. The representations of language thus take on another shape and become the sign of a desiring subject. The latter linguists can designate in many ways – whether it be a figure of God, or even, of themselves insofar as they desire is of little importance; they will, as linguists, have desired.

In this sense, what we said at the start about the love of language can now be seen to be too partial. It is not only the purists who, denying to the real any status as representable, construe it as the object (*a*). For every linguist, in the very heart of representability, an analogous route is open – to recognise in his or her object that in it a subject is making a sign and, without having to represent it further, can by this sign cause his or her desire.

No academic community has to know anything of this moment – in it every linguist remains unrecognised, and whenever several of them gather together, they carefully refrain from talking about it, each of them too doubtful that any other among them could assign it the same features and the same consistency. And moreover, it has to do with something entirely different from what makes them linguists in one another's eyes–rather, perhaps, with what makes them human, those beings who, after discovering themselves to be alike, find themselves not united, but separated.

This is no doubt the source of the motley character which every assembly of linguists preserves in contrast to the scientific community, for in order to guarantee the silence required concerning the nocturnal point of the contraction, one must hold to the most accepted forms of demonstration and formalising notation. But who can not be aware that at any moment, from the very heart of the object delineated, the spectre of truth might not arise, witness to the incompleteness and the process of extraction on which depend both the comportment of theories and the permanence of academic qualifications?

Notes

1. Here Dante should be consulted: 'The inventors of the art of grammar were moved by this consideration, grammar being indeed nothing other than a certain uniformity of language [Language] which does not change in different times and places . . . They invented it, then, out of a fear that, because of the change in language which issues from the will of individuals, we wouldn't be able to understand either not at all or at least imperfectly the authoritative ideas and histories of the ancients' *De Vulgari Eloquentia*, in Robert S. Haller (trans.) and (ed.), *Literary Criticism of Dante Alighieri* (Lincoln: University of Nebraska Press, 1973, I. ix, 11) p. 15.
2. I follow Samuel Beckett here in translating *semblables* as 'likes'. See *Waiting for Godot* (New York: Grove Press, 1954) p. 16, and *En Attendant Godot* (Paris: Minuit, 1952) p. 38, as well as *How It Is* (New York: Grove Press, 1964) p. 37, 'my brotherly likes' for 'mes semblables et frères' in *Comment C'est* (Paris: Minuit, 1961) p. 58. The last is of course an allusion to Baudelaire. (Translator's note.]
3. In the same way that Aristotle's categories determine the modes according to which an object can in general be represented to cognition in a judgement, the grammatical categories do so for language in general. It is thus legitimate for the same term to be customary in both cases.
4. A simple example: the verb *savoir* ('to know'), is, in French, followed by two types of complements, one in *que*, the other in *si*. It would be

tempting to say that the division is syntactic: *que* appears when *savoir* is affirmed; *si* everywhere else, when *savoir* is negated or questioned. This gives the following paradigm:

(a) A sait que B vient   A knows that B is coming
(b) A ne sait pas si B vient   A does not know if B is coming
(c) A sait-il si B vient?   Does A know if B is coming?

But the principle is immediately refuted, since one finds the following:

(d) A ne sait pas que B vient   A does not know that B is coming
(e) A sait-il que B vient?   Does A know that B is coming?

It is not enough, moreover, to have recourse to the subject of the statement or enouncement: the knowledge of the subject A is the same in (b)–(c) as in (d)–(e). This is even clearer, since, to the examples with *que* following non-assertions, one can add examples with *si* following assertions:

(f) A sait (sûrement) si B vient   A surely knows if B is coming

In fact, the key to the paradigm lies in the subject of the utterance or enunciation: everything depends on its knowledge; in (a), it knows and in (f) it does not know that B is coming, the knowledge of the subject of the statement being the same in both cases; and this is the case, *mutatis mutandis*, in every one of the pairs (b)/(d), (c)/(e):*que* implies knowledge and *si* non-knowledge on the part of the subject of the utterance or enunciation, whatever may be the case for the subject of the statement or enouncement.

In this way the distributional irregularities are explained when the subject of the statement and the subject of the utterance coincide in the first person–we do not find alongside of (f):

(g) *je sais si A vient   *I know if A is coming

nor beside (d):

(h) *je ne sais pas que A vient   *I don't know that A is coming

In fact, given the properties of the first person, of the present and of the verb *savoir* ('to know'), the difference between the knowledge of the subject of the utterance or enunciation and that of the subject of the statement which would permit *que* in a negative context and *si* in a positive context would not in this case exist.

If, on the other hand, one introduces a temporal variation allowing once more the knowledge of the two subjects to be separated, while preserving the first person, we find:

(i) je savais déjà à ce   I knew already at that moment
    moment-là si A viendrait   if A would come

    je ne savais pas que   I did not know that A
    A viendrait   would come

On the basis of this example, it becomes apparent how the subject of the utterance permits a regularity to be described, but it can also be seen that nothing is presupposed of it but its existence; of that which, in this existence, makes a subject, there is nothing to be known.

9

Envoy

Today linguistics scarcely arouses interest any more, even to the point of being thought boring. Perhaps it has always been thus with the disciplines which treat of language, save for that time when, the master-word having the figure of the All, structuralism found its justification and its resources in those who seemed to have so effectively established the hold of the All over language. But in our time, the All no longer exerts its attraction, and the inscriptions which it allows readily pass for oppressive. Linguistics is included in this discredit of the all, owing entirely to the monotonous order that it would maintain in minds and in society. Moreover, it considers itself as a science; and indeed, not having instituted any well established technique (one can hardly point to anything but pedagogy which it serves to justify), it is nothing but that and owes its continued existence only to the writings which qualify it. Now, it is well known that the writings of science, sanctioned as they are by the One, give rise to a boredom which is ordinarily covered up and compensated for by the usefulness of the techniques – but, in this case, what use can they be put to?

Linguistics, furthermore, importunes, not that this should be surprising. We have only to recall Freud and his claim about wounded narcissism: Copernican astronomy, he said, and psychoanalysis have this in common – they both make an attack upon narcissism, the first dislodging man from the centre of the universe, the second stealing from him his mastery over his own psyche. It is not difficult to see that the same holds for the grammatical or linguistic point of view. To devote oneself to language in itself, to recognise in it the facets of a real, is to say to speaking beings that, as far as personal experience goes, there is, in language and in every grammatical construction, something which they are neither masters of nor responsible for. Now, this is

137

something which it is hard to accept; for from whence does anyone derive the emblems of their responsibility, if not from the fact of being speaking? Does the gesture by which speaking beings set themselves up as the human race, instance of imaginary mastery in the universe, consist in anything else than in the apprehension of *lalangue* as a distinctive property such that there are some beings without it, and who are thereby excluded from the roster of responsible agents? Establishing the beings who speak as the set of masters can be accomplished then only by correlatively registering *lalangue* as the All.

This is indeed what linguistics does, but it is paradoxically in order to place in the heart of this All the agency which strips the speaking being of all responsibility, of what makes it a man and master of the Universe. This is no doubt the reason why, of those sciences called human, linguistics is the only one which does not lend itself directly to the conditionings demanded by the modern master, and consequently the only one which yields nothing, except to a few charlatans. To unmake man at the very point where man is constituted, to injure the person where the person finds solace, is thus the major offence. One can easily imagine that linguists themselves would find it hard to accept this unflinchingly. As a consequence they can be observed ranging in desperation far from that which gives them their authority, hurrying to patch up, in one way or another, the wounds they have inflicted. There are two recourses currently open: one to meaning – isn't the speaking being at least responsible for what it intends to say, despite the constraints set upon what it actually says? – and the other to society – isn't the speaking being inscribed in it as citizen, responsible for its own declarations, insofar as they affect its fate and that of others? If necessary, moreover, these two recourses can be combined. It suffices to make a reference to ideology and to decipher, both in actual utterances (considered as linguistic practices) and in the operations which analyse them, the social choices carried by meanings.

In this way, an anti-linguistics is constantly being developed, one aimed particularly at helping linguists put up with themselves – sociolinguistics, semantics whether generative or not, ideological inquiries – the names matter little, since it is always a question of reinvesting with its full rights and duties a subject who is its own master and at least responsible for its choices. The Universe can then turn to the music of the spheres, in the hands of the human race, healed of the indescribable wound created by the supposition that language or something in it exceeds its grasp.

This tendency should not, after all, be surprising; can it not be observed in any discourse which deals with the emblems of mastery, psychoanalysis included? Perhaps it is only more constant here, since there are no linguists who do not slip into it at some time or other, either under their own impetus or through the terrorism of universal consensus. This is no doubt because linguistics, insofar as it appertains to science, creates no social bond except through the University; caught in the academic system, linguists must form a community and make themselves exchangeable, insofar as it is possible to do so. This keeps any one of them from being able, *qua* subject, to utter the word which inspires confidence and creates the effect of truth. Nothing other than a secret and not readily collectivisable ethic then is able, among some of them, to set up a barrier against the demands of responsibility.

There is, however, no other way except through importunity to others and to themselves, if linguists are to experience the thrill of satisfaction. For like all scientists – and no doubt unlike the psychoanalyst – they have earned one – the singular jubilation that decipherment procures. Who better than the linguist can in effect within the recesses of a network of the real, seize upon the flash of a sense that no meaning comes to dull? Who, indeed, since the substance of that which the linguist manipulates is made up solely of these shimmerings?

No doubt, once brushed up against, the sense will be found to be assigned to meanings of order and regularity, since such are the features under which linguistics recognises the hold of the All with which it is concerned. No doubt, out of these regularities ranged in order within the constraints of a writing, nothing but boredom can be born, once passion is extinguished (and what can better put it out than the academic style?). But, make no mistake about it, it is in the drawn-out repetition constructed from the symmetry of rules and paradigms that the flash of sense is released which the rule simultaneously stands for and effaces.

In this unique instant, it is no longer the linguist who knows, but *lalangue* which knows through the linguist, for this is the truth of the linguist's competence – not mastery, but subjection and the discovery that *lalangue* knows. The fact that the linguist must immediately spell out this knowledge in a scientific writing is finally of little consequence; in the space of a flash of lightning, nothing can distinguish what will soon take the form of a rule from the merest play on words – Witz or slip of the tongue. What is at stake has the same status as a flicker of sense along the paths of the signifier.[1] So it is indeed the same jubilation which breaks out, so much the more precious in that it touches in the linguist only what makes him or her a speaking being.

Nevertheless it is a happy accident if, while still meeting the demands of style, linguists can from time to time participate in this. Aside from academic exchange which, as we know, is indispensable to them, it is the only justification with some dignity which they can find for writing. But that would entail on their part an unprecedented effort: creating a writing in which the instant the sense arises is not attenuated, but in which also there is no resistance to its being arranged, if this is so desired, in configurations of tables and rules. A writing, then, which dares not speak its name, and grammatical constructions with a double meaning. Nothing, moreover, is easier for anyone who reads a linguist than not to watch for this imperceptible crack where something of a thrill of pleasure is perhaps transcribed, for it is presented under the very features of demonstrative certitude. Furthermore, if the transcription succeeds, the instant in which the sense arises should be nowhere other than in the moment when the linguist has pushed the evidence to the point of conclusion. It is in this same evidence, which justifies the conclusion and demands assent, that the navel of the pleasure should be sought, for those who can read it.[2]

'*Lalangue* knows', such is the assumption of linguists. In spelling out this knowledge in the writing of science, they create the conditions for a thrill in which, by their transcriptions, they invite speaking beings to participate. They have no assurance, however, that these beings will be satisfied with it. For another way is available, as to the knots of the thrill of pleasure and *lalangue*. How better to illuminate it than by a homology of *lalangue* and woman that Lacanian writing generates and that its doctrine interprets?

It all depends on the following: the sexual, where woman, as such, enters, takes its makeup from the existence of *lalangue*; for speaking beings, it is insofar as they are caught in *lalangue* that their inscription, relative to their desire, takes the dramatic form of the sexes. Desire and *lalangue* corrupting one another mutually, whatever relation would come to exist between such beings could not be all written. This is expressed as 'there is no sexual relation', or, also as 'there is no reference or communication save that which is imaginary'. A double entry system is erected, in which can be traced, depending on the direction taken, just as much the loss of the object in the articulation of desire as the illocutionary failing of the subject, supported, hypothetically, by the speaking individual. At each point, the same impossibility can be attested to, for which *lalangue* and woman are but two modes.

From this the following can be observed: *lalangue* justifies no universality; *The language* does not exist, but only this 'several' in which Mallarmé located its failure. Despite the packaged totalisations which the famous parts of speech and levels allow, neither does *The* construction nor *The* word exist. It is the reign of open sets, which however can be counted – the *mille e tre* of Don Juan should come to mind.

Moreover, to this homology, words themselves bear witness – just as in fact woman is not inscribed in the sexual relation except *quoad matrem*, so likewise for *lalangue* with respect to communication. It achieves this end only as mother tongue,[3] exceeding the needs of reference.

It is not difficult to multiply the anecdotes duplicating the core of homology. Better to proceed straight to what is essential, which is that for some, the Other can be presented just as easily in the figure of language as in the figure of woman. Such is the case for Dante, for whom Beatrice and the Italian language assume an identical position – to the point that, if Beatrice takes pleasure, one must hold that for Dante language does so as well. To escape from serving it is thus simply sodomy,[4] Virgil by contrast held up as the model of the perfect lover, he who made himself unflaggingly the instrument of pleasure, of *jouissance*, for a mistress-language.

'Lalangue takes pleasure'' this is the strange notion here set forth. Less strange, however, than one would have first believed, since this is indeed what is required to animate with some tinge of sense the calculations of non-sense which Jakobson, in the footsteps of Saussure, has come to explore. For, despite what one might say, in the calculation of phonemes or metre, there is no need to recognise the slightest demand for order and symmetry; instead, it is a matter of constantly putting the elements subject to the One to the continuous service of an Other who is meant to take pleasure, to have his or her thrill – an other thrill, beyond the thrill, one which is sustained elsewhere by woman, or God. Here, at this infinite point, however, *lalangue* causes the lover, the mystic and the poet to meet.

Here then is the possibility about which linguists as such can know nothing. Everything keeps them from supposing there to be in *lalangue* the slightest thrill, which could serve only to devalue their own. At times, no doubt, a linguist meets a poet and listens to him or her, but hagiography should not mislead us. For could anyone who should happen to read one of the rare testimonies we possess on this point – namely, the obituary dedicated to Maja-kovskij by Jakobson[5] – not but decipher in it a confession? It is upon the silence of those who have served *lalangue* and the thrill it holds that the discourse of linguists is grounded. By a move that has become familiar to us, even if it is in crowning it with laurels, they must banish from the All which alone provides their authori-sation the being who, as speaking, is condemned to the not-all.

This is the price at which linguistics can make itself under-stood – tedious at times in contrast to this Other way that it closes off, often importunate, as a result of confining itself to the very point of an impossible, but not sad, as long as it does not botch the writing of its decipherings. A difficult operation, no doubt, but one which has had its successes – rare, incommensurate with one another, inimitable, dependent on pure chance, they are a testi-mony nonetheless. Once again, for them to be recognised, it is necessary for the speaking being, called upon by the linguist to tolerate itself as such, to accept the minimum – that no one is master of *lalangue*, that a real is insistent therein, that *lalangue* finally knows. Then, so long as the linguist is not wanting in a certain tact, at some point in the learned writings there can be achieved the happy convergence of the rule and the Witz.

Notes

1. From another point of view, all joking which involves language is the registration, by the subject, of a knowledge of *lalangue*. Cf. J. Milner, 'Langage et langue – ou: de quoi rient les locuteurs?'
2. It would be relevant to make a survey of the figures of evidence and to set up a typology of the moments of closure: for Troubetzkoy, complementarity, by which two entities are to be identified by having no common predicate; for Benveniste, the pure difference which separates, from the point of view of a system of relations, two entities all of whose empirical predicates are the same; for Jakobson, the laying

out in terms of symmetry and asymmetry of the disjoint elements; for Chomsky, the deduction of the most erratic series starting from a few minimal writings. Are not the great linguists thus those who succeed in making generally accepted a new figure of evidence – that is to say at one and the same instant an unprecedented trace of their thrill, their *jouissance*?

3. If *lalangue* cannot be represented as maternal, some displacement occurs. This is what is attested to among others by Wolfson, the now celebrated schizophrenic. Not being able to gain access to *lalangue* from the side marked as the mother's, he looked for it on the side of an indefinite combining of various languages. The not-all draws attention to itself hence by the fact that Wolfson found it impossible to complete the entireties, the alls of a word and phoneme. The logic of the all which Deleuze not long ago recognised in this (see introduction to Louis Wolfson, *Le Schizo et les Langues*, (Paris: Gallimard, 1970, p. 20) is thus consubstantial with the sexual inscription, which he then made the rule of psychosis (p. 23).

4. Brunetto Latini, Italian writing in French and praising this language, is consequently condemned with the sodomites to punishment by fire. On the question of this 'spiritual' sodomy, cf. A. Pezard, *Dante sous la pluie de feu* (Paris: Vrin, 1950) pp. 294–312. The congruence of the figure of the woman and that of *lalangue* could have come to Dante's attention through the troubadours, for among them courtly love is linked to hermeticism – to compensate for the absence of relation, to feign creating, by choice, an obstacle to it, whether through the inaccessible Lady or by an obscure reference.

5. 'La Génération Qui a Gaspillé ses Poètes' in *Questions de Poétique*, pp. 73–101.